THE CINNAMON CLUB
SEAFOOD
COOKBOOK

Thank you

Vivek Singh

Publisher and Project Editor Jon Croft Commissioning Editor Meg Avent Editor Jane Middleton
Creative direction and design Ian Middleton at Design United Worldwide Photographer Jean Cazals Stylist Sue Rowlands
ISBN 1 904573 41 X
First published in Great Britain in 2006 by Absolute Press, Scarborough House, 29 James Street West, Bath BA1 2BT
T: 44 (0) 1225 316013 F: 44 (0) 1225 445836 email: info@absolutepress.co.uk Website: www.absolutepress.co.uk

A CIP catalogue record of this book is available from the British Library
Printed and bound by Lego, Italy

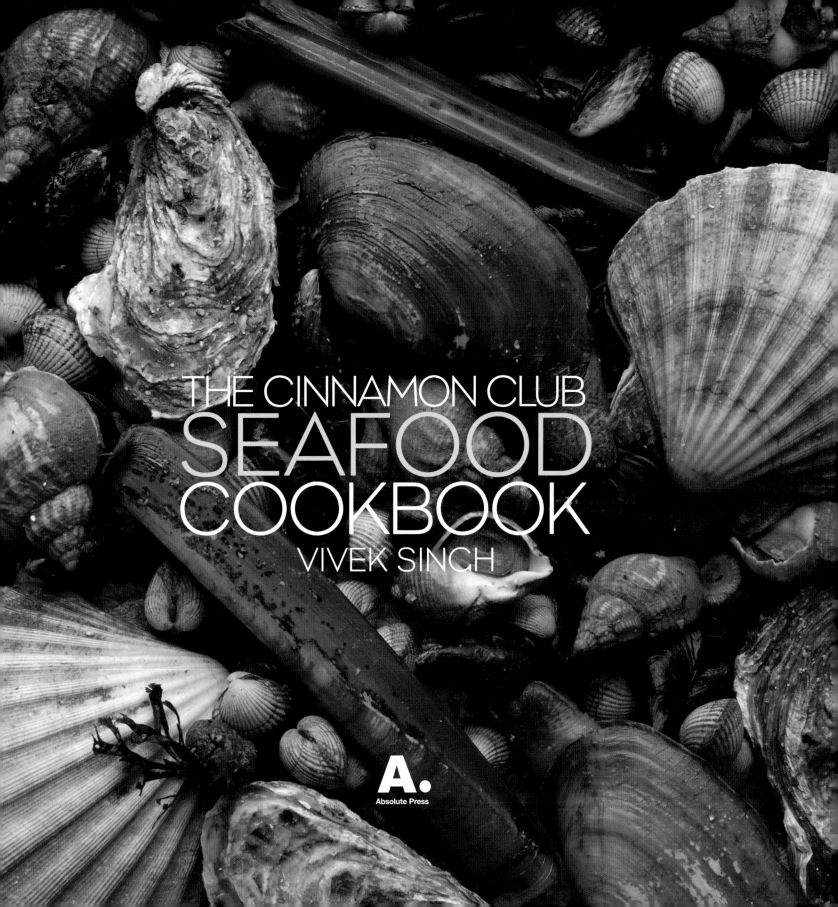

THE CINNAMON CLUB
SEAFOOD
COOKBOOK

VIVEK SINGH

A.

Absolute Press

ACKNOWLEDGMENTS

FOR ARCHANA, MY WIFE FOR SACRIFICING NUMEROUS WEEKENDS, THE BOYS IN THE KITCHEN, JEAN CAZALS WHO MAKES THE BOOK LOOK SEXY, THE DESIGN BY IAN MIDDLETON FOR BRINGING METHOD TO THE MADNESS, ESHAAN, MY SON FOR MISSING OUT ON BREAKFAST ON SATURDAY MORNINGS, HARI KUMAR FOR LOOKING AFTER EVERYTHING ELSE, IQBAL FOR INSPIRATION, JON CROFT FOR HIS BELIEF IN THE CINNAMON CLUB, LAURENT FOR HIS SUPPORT, JANE MIDDLETON WITHOUT WHOM THERE WOULD HAVE BEEN A MILLION MISTAKES, PRATAP CHAHAL FOR BEING THE GUINEA PIG, RAKESH NAIR WITHOUT WHOM THIS BOOK WOULD NOT HAVE HAPPENED, THE TEAM AT THE CINNAMON CLUB WHO MAKE US WHAT WE ARE, MARCO PIERRE WHITE FOR WHITE HEAT.

SPECIAL THANKS

There are two colleagues without whose help this book would not have been possible. First, Rakesh Ravindran Nair, who has been involved right from the initial compilation of recipes to testing and photography. Besides being a chef, Rakesh has a Masters degree in Mathematics and is a qualified computer professional. He has been at the Cinnamon Club since 2003 and seafood is his passion. He is one of the generation of 'thinking chefs' who, with their ability to combine the best of both worlds, will take Indian cuisine to the next level.

Secondly, Hari Kumar has assisted in organising all the ingredients, recipe trials and photo shoots. Hari has been at the Cinnamon Club since 2001 and embodies the ethos of evolved Indian cooking and all the values that are part of our philosophy at the Cinnamon Club.

Together, these two are frontrunners in the new generation of chefs, who will have an important role to play in the Indian cuisine of tomorrow.

Rakesh
Ravindran Nair

Hari Kumar

SOME NOTES FOR AMERICAN READERS

In the recipes, American measures are given in brackets after the metric measures.
Below are the American terms for some of the ingredients and equipment used in this book.

baking parchment = wax paper
baking sheet = cookie sheet
beetroot = beets
caster sugar = superfine sugar
celeriac = celery root
cling film = plastic wrap
coriander = cilantro (when referring to the green, leafy herb rather than the seeds)
cornflour = cornstarch
double cream = heavy cream
frying pan = skillet

Greek yoghurt = thick plain yoghurt
grill = broiler
grilled = broiled
groundnut oil = peanut oil
hard-boiled egg = hard-cooked egg
kitchen paper = paper towels
lemon sole = English sole, flounder
monkfish = anglerfish
pepper, red or green = bell pepper, red or green
plaice = flounder, sole

plain flour = all-purpose flour
prawns = shrimp
red mullet = goatfish
sea bream = snapper
shrimps = very small shrimp
sieve = strainer
single cream = light cream
spring onion = scallion
tomato purée = tomato paste

INTRODUCTION

Every now and then something happens that completely changes the way you look at things. Reading a rare copy of Marco Pierre White's *White Heat* with a likeminded chef in Calcutta in 1997 had this effect on me. The energy conveyed through its text and pictures portrayed our profession in a light we had never seen before and filled us with a sense of pride. It had a lasting impact on my career and opened my eyes to a world that I had not known existed. Inspirational!

When I arrived in London in December 2000 to become head chef at the Cinnamon Club, one of the first things I did was visit Billingsgate fish market. This, too, had a profound effect on my cooking. There was so much produce available that I had never come across before – both local and exotic. It was an overwhelming experience, exciting, stimulating and challenging all at the same time, and I was immensely pleased that I had not arrived in the country with a fixed set of ideas for what to cook. I realised that I was going to have a lot of fun putting the Cinnamon Club's first menu together. We had already decided to use top-quality fish and meat with traditional Indian spicing and techniques but it had never occurred to me that there would be so many possibilities. Iqbal Wahhab, founder of the Cinnamon Club, suggested that we change the menu daily in order to respond best to the markets and availability. This became fundamental to our cooking philosophy and to our approach to seafood in particular. As we worked hard to set up the restaurant, our minds were kept busy trying to think up new dishes with different spicing, sauces and accompaniments. So much so that by the end of the first year we had used 76 different varieties of fish and seafood on our menu.

FISH AND SEAFOOD IN INDIA

Most of us had only ever had access to three or four species of fish and seafood in restaurants in India. Distribution and transport facilities there are still far from what you might expect. The lack of infrastructure makes it financially unviable to transport seafood too far, and generally fish can be enjoyed only within 50 kilometres or so of its place of catch. Whatever little infrastructure exists is geared up for export to other countries and this phenomenon has had a lasting effect on fish cookery in India, both in homes and in restaurants.

Chefs from northern India rarely get the opportunity to work with anything other than prawns, pomfret, bekti and a local freshwater fish called singara. Salmon, and very occasionally sole and scallops, are imported and considered very exotic. More often than not, though, they are reserved for use in French or Chinese restaurants, and rarely find their way into Indian kitchens. Chefs working in the south are more fortunate, especially if they are close enough to the coast to get daily supplies of fresh fish. Most restaurants in Bombay and Goa serve an abundance of fish and seafood. The coast of Kerala is one of the richest sources, with varieties such as tuna, mackerel, spotted bream, sardines, king prawns and crabs. Even away from the coast, Kerala has backwaters that extend for miles and are home to many types of fish and shellfish not seen elsewhere – eel, pearl-spot, cockles and conch, plus freshwater prawns and crabs. Fish and seafood cooking is also taken quite seriously in Bengal, Bihar and Orissa, which enjoy substantial supplies throughout the year.

Perhaps because of its relative scarcity, fish is considered auspicious in many parts of India and is served at religious and social celebrations. Traditionally, Brahmins do not consume any kind of flesh. However, in most Bengali households, fish is considered acceptable and is part of daily diet.
In most North Indian restaurants, fish and seafood are included on the menu purely to balance it out. The spicing is designed to mask the flavours of fish that is past its prime. Lots of strong spices are used together and the fish is cut into unrecognisably small pieces, then cooked for a prolonged period in a large amount of sauce so that you simply can't taste anything! This, of course, is a world apart from the fish cookery in parts of southern India – especially Kerala, where the spicing is fresh, the cooking light and flavoursome and the fish divine.

THE CINNAMON CLUB PHILOSOPHY

Ingredients are the key to any successful cuisine. Good-quality fresh ingredients need very little done to them to taste good. Once you've sourced the best produce, you can use techniques and spicing that allow the flavours to express themselves. It is often a question of understanding what cooking process your ingredients need and then doing just that, rather than following a blanket cooking method for everything. Essentially it's a matter of respect for your ingredients. The skill lies in recognising quality and freshness and learning to leave well alone!

With the range and quality of ingredients available to us now, we need to look closely at some of the things that are traditionally done. At the Cinnamon Club, we decided that quality, seasonality and freshness would be paramount in everything we cooked. With a little experimentation, we devised some techniques that enabled us to incorporate the amazing range of fresh seafood available in London into our cooking.

One of the most important steps was our decision to serve fish in large, portion-sized pieces rather than cut into small dice, as is the norm in Indian cooking. This meant we could control its cooking much better and it also allowed for better appreciation of the textures and flavours. We also made a conscious decision to leave the skin on fish where possible. The benefits are numerous. It helps hold the fish together during cooking, prevents it becoming dry and adds another texture to the dish. Another break-through was the double-marinade technique we developed for tandoori-style cook-ing. The first marinade draws out excess moisture from the fish, enabling the second marinade to coat the fish better, thereby protecting it from the intense heat of the tandoor. The resulting dish has much more upfront spicing and the fish has firm, succulent flesh.

Looking to the Far East, we incorporated cooking styles such as stir-fries and dumplings in our cooking. At the same time we added Western techniques such as roasting, searing and grilling to our repertoire of traditional Indian cooking methods.

Taking the trouble to understand our ingredients, and looking afresh at traditional cooking techniques, helped us come up with a repertoire of dishes and flavouring combinations that opened up a world of possibility to us.

CHANGING TIMES

I have always maintained that, apart from the quality of its ingredients and the creativity of its practitioners, adaptability is the key to the success of any cuisine. All great cuisines have at some time or another had someone come along and turn convention on its head. I call these people 'thinking chefs', and they have the ability to redefine the cuisine of the future.

Gone are the days when a chef's skill was judged on how well he or she was able to mask the flavours of produce. Now chefs are judged on their ability to bring out the best in their ingredients.

There are so many factors affecting the way we eat now – changes in farming and production methods, health scares, debates over food miles and other environmental issues, plus a new appreciation of the value of local, seasonal cooking – that we are constantly having to reassess our approach to food. Our ability to adapt our cuisine to changing times, with a view to keeping it relevant, has never been more important.

Vivek Singh, May 2006

BUYING AND PREPARING FISH

When shopping for fish and shellfish, remember the fresher the better. Below are some of the things to look out for to make sure your fish is absolutely fresh. A good fishmonger should be able to tell you where and when the fish were caught. If possible, shop at a fishmonger's that's always busy – then the chances are that the fish has not been sitting around for too long.

- Fresh fish should smell of the sea, not of fish. If it's fresh and briny, you're in for some good eating. Walk away if it's stinky and fishy.
- The flesh should feel firm to the touch and, if pressed lightly, should spring back. If your fingers leave a depression, then the fish is no longer fresh. If you can twist a fish enough for it to kiss its tail, it is well past its prime!
- The eyes should be clear and bright, not sunken and dull.
- The skin should be shiny and bright, with no discolouration or damage.
- If possible, lift up the gills to check that they are bright red underneath. Darkening indicates that the fish is not fresh.
- If the fish has large scales, they should be firmly attached, not flaking off.
- Fish fillets should be firm, should smell fresh and have bright skin. There should be no obvious bruising or damage to the flesh.
- Molluscs and crustaceans should smell sweet and briny.
- Bivalves such as mussels, clams, oysters and scallops should be alive when bought. Avoid any with broken or chipped shells.
- Live lobsters and crabs should be moving strongly. Cooked ones should feel heavy for their size.
- Crustaceans should have no apparent bruising or damage to the shells. Any blackening at the joints means they are not fresh.

Eat your fish as soon as possible after purchase – especially fillets or steaks, which deteriorate quicker than whole fish. Fresh fish needs to be tightly wrapped and kept very well chilled, at around 0°C (32°F). Any colder than this, however, and it will begin to freeze. Whole fish store best when gutted, which your fishmonger should be able to do for you. If freezing fish, wrap it well in plastic film or freezer bags and place in the coldest part of the freezer; depending upon the freshness of the fish when you bought it, it could keep for up to three months. Thaw slowly in the fridge before use.

To store bivalves and crustaceans, cover them with a damp cloth or thick paper and place in the fridge, where they should keep for up to two days. Live shellfish need to stay moist but they also need to breathe, so never wrap them in plastic or submerge in fresh water.

Cleaning

To scale a fish, hold it by the tail and use the back of a knife (or ideally a fish scaler) to scrape towards the head.

To remove the gills, place the fish on its back, open the gill flap, gently pull the gills out through the flap, then cut and discard. Trim off the fins with a pair of scissors. To gut a whole fish, make a slit in the stomach and pull out all the entrails, then rinse the fish thoroughly under cold running water.

Filleting

Make a cut behind the head, then move a very sharp knife along the backbone, cutting into the flesh with clean sweeping strokes as close to the backbone as possible, moving towards the tail. Work your way through the flesh till you reach the other end, then cut to separate the fillet from the bones. Repeat with the other fillet.

Skinning fish fillets

Put the fillet on a board, skin-side down, with the tail end nearest you. Make a small cut across the tail end, without cutting right through, to release the skin. Then take hold of the end bit of skin with one hand, place the knife between the skin and the flesh with the other hand and gently work it along the fillet towards the head end, easing the flesh off the skin and holding the skin taut.

Shelling and de-veining prawns

Pull the head off the body if it is still attached. Peel the shell away from the body with your fingers, then make a shallow cut along the back of the prawn and pull out the dark intestinal vein with the tip of the knife.

Cleaning mussels

Tap any open mussels with the back of a knife and they should close. Discard any that don't. To de-beard them, hold the mussel with a towel and yank the beard (also known as the byssal threads) towards the hinge end to pull it out. Then scrub the mussels thoroughly under cold running water to remove any dirt or grit.

BASICS

GINGER PASTE

Makes about 6 tablespoons

175g (6 ounces) fresh ginger, peeled
5 tablespoons water

Chop up the ginger and process it to a paste with the water in a food processor or blender. The paste will keep for 1 week in the fridge.

GARLIC PASTE

Makes about 6 tablespoons

175g (6 ounces) garlic, peeled
5 tablespoons water

Chop up the garlic and process it to a paste with the water in a food processor or blender. The paste will keep for 1 week in the fridge, but if you substitute oil for water it should keep for 2 weeks.

MACE AND CARDAMOM POWDER

¼ nutmeg
40g (1½ ounces) mace blades
50g (2 ounces) green cardamom pods

Grate the nutmeg or pound it with a mortar and pestle to break it up. Dry all the spices in a microwave for 30 seconds, then grind them to a fine powder. Store in an airtight container and use within 3–4 days.

BOILED CASHEW PASTE

Makes about 400g (14 ounces)

200g (7 ounces) cashew nuts
1 blade of mace
1 green cardamom pod
300ml (1¼ cups) water

Soak the cashew nuts in enough water to cover for 10 minutes, then drain. Put them in a pan with the mace, cardamom and water, bring to the boil and simmer for 25 minutes. Remove from the heat and leave to cool. Blend to a smooth paste in a food processor or blender with 100ml (scant ½ cup) water. The paste will keep for 4 days in the fridge.

RAJASTHANI SPICE PASTE

2 tablespoons mustard oil
   (or sunflower oil)
2 tablespoons ghee or clarified butter
1 large onion, sliced
6 garlic cloves, chopped
20 cloves
10 green cardamom pods
1 tablespoon coriander seeds
1 teaspoon black peppercorns
1 tablespoon fennel seeds
150g (5 ounces) fresh coriander (root, stem or leaf), chopped
1 teaspoon salt
150g (2/3 cup) Greek yoghurt

Heat the oil in a heavy-based frying pan until smoking, then add the ghee or clarified butter. Add the sliced onion and cook until softened but not browned. Add the garlic and cook for a few minutes, until it starts to colour. Add the cloves, cardamom, coriander seeds, peppercorns and fennel seeds in that order and stir quickly over a high heat for a couple of minutes, taking care that the spices do not burn. Stir in the chopped coriander and salt, then remove from the heat and leave to cool.

Transfer the mixture to a food processor or blender, add the yoghurt and blend to a paste.

GARAM MASALA

There are many versions of garam masala; this is a good basic one. It is generally added to dishes towards the end of cooking to impart flavour, not to add heat as its name might suggest (garam means hot and masala means mix).

I would always recommend making your own garam masala if possible. Commercial blends use a larger proportion of the cheaper spices and less of the more expensive aromatic ones, such as cardamom and cinnamon.

50g (2 ounces) coriander seeds
50g (2 ounces) cumin seeds
20 green cardamom pods
10 cinnamon sticks, about 2.5cm (1 inch) long
2 tablespoons cloves
10 blades of mace
10 black cardamom pods
½ nutmeg
1 tablespoon black peppercorns
4 bay leaves

Put all the ingredients on a baking tray and place in a low oven (about 110°C/225°F/Gas Mark ¼) for 3–5 minutes; this intensifies the flavours (alternatively you could dry the spices in a microwave for 20 seconds or so). Grind everything to a powder in a spice grinder, then sift the mixture to remove any husks or large particles. Store in an airtight container and use within 2 weeks.

The sediment is the cooked milk solids and should be carefully removed and discarded. The golden liquid solidifies when cool but should stay creamy, like soft margarine. Store in the fridge.

BOILED RICE

Serves 6–8

500g (2½ cups) basmati rice
1 tablespoon vegetable or corn oil
a large pinch of salt

Soak the rice in cold water for about 10 minutes, then drain. Bring a large pan of water to the boil with the oil and add the salt. Add the rice and simmer, uncovered, for 9–12 minutes, until the grains give way when you press them between your fingertips but are still slightly firm in the centre (al dente).

Remove from the heat and drain through a large colander. To prevent further cooking, you could pour cold water over the rice, or simply spread it out in a large baking tray and leave to cool.

ROASTING (AND CRUSHING) SEEDS

If a recipe requires seeds to be roasted, put them in a moderately hot frying pan or under the grill and roast for a minute or two, until they are just dried but not coloured. To crush them, remove from the heat and pound together in a mortar and pestle, until the seeds are crushed but still coarse enough to be identified separately. If you want to grind the seeds to a powder, the best way to do this is in a spice grinder.

GHEE

Cooking butter in this way stops it going rancid and also enables it to withstand high temperatures and constant reheating. Correctly made, ghee will keep in the fridge for several years.

Place 250g (1 cup) unsalted butter in a heavy-based pan and heat gently until it melts. Bring to the boil, then reduce the heat and simmer for 20–30 minutes, skimming off the froth from the surface, until the sediment has settled at the bottom and separated from the clear, golden ghee.

CANAPES

WHITEBAIT IN GARLIC AND PEPPER BATTER

SRI LANKAN-STYLE TUNA SPRING ROLLS

TAMARIND RICE SUSHI ROLLS

SWORDFISH WITH COCONUT, CHILLI AND MUSTARD

BENGALI-STYLE FISHCAKES WITH RAISINS

SOUTH INDIAN SHRIMP PICKLE

KING PRAWN CUTLETS WITH CORN AND RICE CRUST

CHARGRILLED GROUPER WITH PEANUT SAUCE

PRAWNS ON TOAST

TAWA PARATHAS FILLED WITH CRAB AND PRAWN

STIR-FRIED KING PRAWNS WITH DRIED CHILLI, GARLIC AND SOY

SPICED SPIDER CRAB IN FILO PASTRY WITH PLUM CHUTNEY

WHITEBAIT IN GARLIC AND PEPPER BATTER

SERVES 4

Whitebait and sprats can be used interchangeably in this recipe, which makes a great nibble for cocktail parties. It goes well with any mayonnaise-based dip.

Wash the whitebait in a large bowl of water to remove any sand or dirt, then drain through a sieve. Spread the fish out on kitchen paper to remove excess moisture.

Mix all the ingredients for the batter together until smooth and thick. Add the whitebait, mix well and set aside for 10 minutes.

Heat the oil in a deep-fat fryer or a large, deep saucepan and drop the whitebait in one after another to prevent them sticking together (do this in batches so as not to overcrowd the pan). Fry for about 2 minutes, until crisp, stirring occasionally. Drain on kitchen paper and serve straight away.

500g (1 pound 2 ounces) whitebait
oil for deep-frying

For the batter:
2 tablespoons gram flour
2 tablespoons cornflour
2 teaspoons salt
1 teaspoon Ginger Paste (see page 12)
1 tablespoon Garlic Paste (see page 12)
2 teaspoons red chilli powder
½ teaspoon black onion seeds
1 teaspoon black peppercorns, crushed
1cm (½-inch) piece of fresh ginger, finely chopped
1 tablespoon chopped fresh coriander
juice of 2 lemons
3 tablespoons water

SRI LANKAN-STYLE TUNA SPRING ROLLS

SERVES 8–10

There is a southern Indian version of this recipe that is sold as a snack between meals. I prefer this Sri Lankan one – it is a touch spicier and uses pandan leaves, which lend a special flavour. The spring rolls are rolled in breadcrumbs before frying and served with Seeni Sambal, a hot and sweet onion marmalade. Serve as canapés or as a starter.

Place the tuna on a baking sheet, sprinkle with the salt, pepper and oil and cook for 6–8 minutes in an oven preheated to 180°C/350°F/Gas Mark 4. Remove from the oven, leave to cool and then flake with a fork.

To make the batter, put the flour and salt into a bowl, add the egg and oil, then gradually whisk in the milk until smooth. Leave to rest for 20 minutes.

Meanwhile, make the filling. Heat the oil in a frying pan, add the crushed ginger and garlic and stir until they release their fragrance. Add the onion, green chillies, curry leaves, pandan leaf and cinnamon stick and sauté for 5–6 minutes, until the onion is golden brown. Add the salt and pepper and the flaked tuna and sauté for 2 minutes. Add the mashed potato, ground cardamom and lime juice and mix everything together.

Remove from the heat and leave to cool. Take out the pieces of pandan leaf and discard them.

To make the pancakes, heat a crêpe pan or a non-stick frying pan (there's no need to oil it), add enough batter to cover the base thinly and cook until lightly coloured underneath. Flip the pancake over and cook the other side, then turn out on to a plate. Repeat with the remaining batter to make 8–10 pancakes. Dust the pancakes with the cornflour as you stack them up, to prevent them sticking together.

To make the spring rolls, place 2 tablespoons of the filling towards the centre of each pancake in a cylindrical shape and then tuck in 3 sides of the pancake over it. Brush the edge of the open end with a little beaten egg and roll the pancake up.

Dip each roll in beaten egg and coat in the breadcrumbs. Heat the oil for deep-frying to 180°C/350°F, add the spring rolls and fry until golden brown (you will need to do this in 2 or 3 batches). Remove and drain on kitchen paper. Cut each spring roll in half and then in half again diagonally. Serve with the Seeni Sambal.

500g (1 pound 2 ounces) fresh tuna loin, cut into 4–5 steaks
½ teaspoon salt
½ teaspoon black peppercorns, crushed
1 tablespoon vegetable oil
Seeni Sambal (see page 114), to serve

For the batter:
125g (1 scant cup) plain flour
a pinch of salt
½ egg, beaten
1½ teaspoons vegetable oil
200ml (⅞ cup) milk
1½ teaspoons cornflour

For the filling:
3 tablespoons vegetable oil
2.5cm (1-inch) piece of fresh ginger, crushed
6 garlic cloves, crushed
1 large red onion, chopped
2 green chillies, chopped
1 sprig of fresh curry leaves
1 pandan leaf, cut into 2.5cm (1-inch) pieces
5cm (2-inch) piece of cinnamon stick
1 teaspoon salt
1 teaspoon black peppercorns, crushed
1 medium potato, boiled and mashed
seeds from 4 green cardamom pods, ground in a mortar and pestle
juice of 1 lime

To finish the spring rolls:
2 eggs, beaten
100g (1 cup) dried breadcrumbs for coating
oil for deep-frying

TAMARIND RICE SUSHI ROLLS

MAKES 30

300g (1½ cups) sushi rice
900ml (3¾ cups) water
3½ tablespoons rice wine vinegar
½ teaspoon salt
1 tablespoon sugar

For the tamarind glaze:
2 teaspoons vegetable oil
1 teaspoon black mustard seeds
150g (⅔ cup) tamarind paste
150ml (⅔ cup) water
1 tablespoon sugar
½ teaspoon red chilli powder

For the spicy mustard:
75g (⅓ cup) wholegrain mustard
1 tablespoon mustard oil
1cm (½-inch) piece of fresh ginger, finely chopped
1 green chilli, finely chopped
1 tablespoon distilled malt vinegar
1½ teaspoons sugar

For the filling:
1 mango, peeled, pitted and sliced into strips 2mm (¹⁄₁₂ inch) thick
1 cucumber, sliced into strips 2mm (¹⁄₁₂ inch) thick
120g (4 ounces) raw tuna, sliced into strips 2mm (¹⁄₁₂ inch) thick

a pinch each of salt, ground cardamom, ground cumin and red chilli powder
juice of ½ lemon

To finish:
2 tablespoons each of blue poppy seeds, sesame seeds and melon seeds, roasted in a dry frying pan
6 large rectangles of banana leaf
a little mustard
1–2 tablespoons Japanese pickled ginger

This is a fun dish to make. It started out when we were playing about with some leftover tamarind rice and it worked so well that we put it on the menu. It's worth noting that your fish should be absolutely fresh.

Put the rice and water in a pan and bring to the boil. Cover tightly and simmer gently for 10–15 minutes, until tender. Spread the rice out on a tray to cool. Bring the rice wine vinegar, salt and sugar to the boil in a pan, pour them over the rice and fold in gently. For the glaze, heat the oil in a pan and add the mustard seeds. When they pop, add the tamarind paste and water. Bring to the boil, add the sugar and chilli and boil for 3–4 minutes. Lower the heat and simmer until reduced to a thick glaze. Cool, then fold into the rice.

For the spicy mustard, put the wholegrain mustard in a bowl. Heat the mustard oil in a pan and add the ginger and chilli. Remove from the heat immediately and stir into the mustard. Add the vinegar and sugar, then chill.

To assemble the sushi, mix together all the ingredients for the filling. Divide the rice into 6. Lay a large piece of cling film on a flat surface and, with wet fingers, place one portion of rice in the middle. Flatten it into a rectangle about 1cm (½ inch) thick. In the middle of the rice, arrange some of the tuna strips in a horizontal line, then arrange some mango and cucumber on either side.

Pick up the side of the cling film nearest you and use it to start to fold the rice over the filling, peeling back the cling film as you go. Lift and roll the rice a second and third time until you have a cylindrical shape and the filling is completely enclosed. Then wrap the roll in the cling film and twist the ends like a bonbon. Holding the ends tightly, roll the package on the work surface to get a perfectly round cylinder. Repeat with the remaining portions of rice. Chill for 10 minutes.

To serve, unwrap the sushi and roll it evenly in the roasted seed mixture. With a knife dipped in hot water, cut each roll into 5 slices. Place a piece of banana leaf down the centre of each of 6 large plates with a little mustard at the top of each one. Arrange 6 sushi slices on each banana leaf and place a few strips of pickled ginger on them.

SWORDFISH WITH COCONUT, CHILLI AND MUSTARD

SERVES 4

This rather unusual dish is cooked by the fishing community in Tamil Nadu, where it is often served as one of the many accompaniments to a big meal or simply on its own as a snack. The double cooking method is also unusual but it imparts a unique texture to the dish. Instead of swordfish, you could use shark or marlin.

Serve on its own as a party snack or on bread as a starter or canapé.

Pat the fish dry on kitchen paper. Rub the salt and half the turmeric over the fish and set aside for 30 minutes.

Put the fish in a saucepan, add enough water to cover, then place over a medium heat, cover and bring to a slow boil. Simmer until the fish is just done. Leave to cool, then remove from the liquid and discard the skin and bones. Using a fork, break up the fish into flakes.

Heat the oil in a large, deep frying pan or a wok and add the mustard seeds. When they begin to crackle, add the dried chillies, curry leaves and garlic and sauté until the garlic turns golden brown. Add the onions and sauté until soft. Add the green chillies and ground spices, including the remaining turmeric, and sauté for a minute longer. Now add the flaked fish and the salt and stir-fry over a high heat until the fish is firm and crisp. Add the grated coconut and stir for a minute. Add the lemon juice, sprinkle with the coriander and remove from the heat.

500g (I pound 2 ounces) shark, swordfish or marlin, cleaned and cut into 4 steaks
I teaspoon salt
I teaspoon ground turmeric
4 tablespoons vegetable or corn oil
I teaspoon mustard seeds
6 dried red chillies
20 fresh curry leaves
6 garlic cloves, crushed
2 large onions, finely chopped
4 green chillies, chopped
2 teaspoons red chilli powder
I teaspoon ground coriander seeds
I teaspoon ground cumin seeds
2 teaspoons salt
80g (I cup) grated fresh coconut
juice of 2 lemons
I tablespoon chopped fresh coriander

BENGALI-STYLE FISHCAKES WITH RAISINS

This is a great little snack from west Bengal. I have very happy memories of eating these as a child – including raisins was our neighbour's way of getting us to like fish!

To make the spice mix, roast all the ingredients in a dry frying pan and then blitz them to a powder in a food processor. Set aside.

To make the fishcakes, put the pieces of cod in a pan and add a couple of tablespoons of water. Add the salt and 1 teaspoon of the turmeric, then cover and braise lightly over a medium heat for about 5–6 minutes, until the fish is just cooked. Remove from the pan and pat dry on kitchen paper. Gently flake the fish with a fork and set aside. Boil the liquid left in the pan until it has reduced to about a tablespoon.

Heat the oil in a large frying pan and add the bay leaves and cumin seeds. When they release their flavour, add the onion and sauté until golden brown. Add the ginger and garlic pastes, followed by the chilli powder and the remaining turmeric, and sauté for a minute. Now add the fish, ginger, green chillies and mashed potato and stir gently to mix them with the spices. Add the reserved cooking liquid. Sprinkle in the spice mix powder, add the raisins and coriander and mix well. Finally, add the beetroot, then remove from the heat and leave to cool.

Divide the mixture into 8 portions and shape into balls. Mix the breadcrumbs with the fennel seeds and black onion seeds. Dust the fishcakes with the flour, dip them in the beaten eggs and then roll them in the breadcrumb mixture until thoroughly coated. Flatten slightly and deep-fry in hot oil for about 2 minutes, until golden brown. Drain on kitchen paper and serve straight away, with salad and some mustardy mayonnaise.

SERVES 4

500g (1 pound 2 ounces) cod fillet, skinned and cut into 4–5 pieces
1 teaspoon salt
1½ teaspoons ground turmeric
3 tablespoons vegetable or corn oil
2 bay leaves
½ teaspoon cumin seeds
1 large onion, chopped
1 teaspoon Ginger Paste (see page 12)
1 teaspoon Garlic Paste (see page 12)
1 teaspoon red chilli powder
1cm (½-inch) piece of fresh ginger, finely chopped
2 green chillies, finely chopped
1 large potato, boiled and mashed
1 tablespoon raisins
2 tablespoons chopped fresh coriander
1 small cooked beetroot, cut into 5mm (¼-inch) dice
oil for deep-frying

For the spice mix:
1 tablespoon coriander seeds
1 teaspoon cumin seeds
seeds from 4 green cardamom pods
1 cinnamon stick

For coating:
200g (3½ cups) breadcrumbs
½ teaspoon fennel seeds
½ teaspoon black onion seeds
25g (⅙ cup) plain flour
2 eggs, beaten

SOUTH INDIAN SHRIMP PICKLE

SERVES 10-12

If ever you end up with too many shrimps, this is a useful way of preserving them. The recipe comes from the Keralan fishing community, which traditionally would pickle the leftover little shrimps after they'd sold the rest of their catch. They are delicious served cold with drinks, either on crisps, toasted bread chips or simply on their own.

To make the spice paste, whiz all the ingredients together to a smooth paste in a blender or food processor.

Heat the oil in a large frying pan, add the onions and sauté until golden brown. Add the green chillies and the spice paste and stir for a minute or two, until the oil separates from the mixture. Add the shrimps and sauté for 3–4 minutes.

Add the salt, sugar, tamarind and vinegar and cook for 4–6 minutes, until the fat comes to the surface. Mix in the coriander, then remove from the heat and leave to cool. Transfer to a container and chill – it tastes better if left for a day. Stored in an airtight jar in the fridge, it should keep for months.

4 tablespoons vegetable or corn oil
2 red onions, chopped
2 green chillies, slit open lengthways
500g (I pound 2 ounces) shrimps (or small prawns), peeled
2 teaspoons salt
I teaspoon sugar
3 tablespoons tamarind paste
I tablespoon malt vinegar
I tablespoon chopped fresh coriander

For the spice paste:
10 dried red chillies
I tablespoon cumin seeds
I tablespoon black peppercorns
2.5cm (I-inch) piece of fresh ginger, chopped
4 garlic cloves, peeled
2 tablespoons malt vinegar

KING PRAWN CUTLETS WITH CORN AND RICE CRUST

SERVES 4-6

These popular Bengali snacks are just prawns that have been flattened out, or 'butterflied', then coated in a spiced batter. The reason they are called cutlets is probably because they are coated in crumbs, like 'chops' or 'cutlets' are in Bengal.

Slice each prawn down through the back, taking care not to cut all the way through, then open it out flat to 'butterfly' it. Pat dry on kitchen paper.

Mix all the ingredients for the marinade together in a shallow dish, then add the prawns and leave to marinate for 15–20 minutes. Drain off the juices, then add the green chillies, chilli flakes, onion seeds, fennel seeds, carom seeds, coriander, flour and egg to the prawns, mixing the spices in well but being careful not to break up the prawns.

Now mix together the rice flakes, cornflakes and breadcrumbs in a shallow dish. Dip the prawns in the mixture, pressing with the palms of your hands to keep them flattened and to ensure the crumbs stick on.

Heat some oil to 180°C/350°F in a deep-fat fryer or a large, deep saucepan. Add the prawns, in batches, and fry for 3–4 minutes, until golden and crisp. Drain on kitchen paper to remove excess oil. Sprinkle with the chaat masala and serve with the lemon wedges, plus a mustardy mayonnaise, tomato ketchup or sweet chilli sauce.

12–18 raw king prawns, peeled and
   deveined, with the tail shell left intact
2 green chillies, very finely chopped
1 teaspoon crushed chilli flakes
½ teaspoon onion seeds
1 teaspoon fennel seeds
1 teaspoon carom (ajowan) seeds
1 tablespoon chopped fresh coriander
1 tablespoon plain flour
1 egg
oil for deep-frying
1 teaspoon chaat masala
lemon wedges, to serve

For the marinade:
1½ teaspoons Ginger Paste (see page 12)
1½ teaspoons Garlic Paste (see page 12)
juice of 1 lemon
1 teaspoon red chilli powder
2 teaspoons salt

For the coating:
3 tablespoons pressed rice flakes
   (pawa)
5 tablespoons cornflakes, lightly
   crushed
2 tablespoons coarse breadcrumbs

CHARGRILLED GROUPER WITH PEANUT SAUCE

SERVES 4

Here is a very simple recipe, which draws its inspiration from Thai cooking. In another version of this dish, the pieces of fish are wrapped in pandan leaves and grilled.

For the marinade, blitz together the garlic, ginger and lemongrass in a food processor, or pound them together in a pestle and mortar. Mix them with the remaining marinade ingredients and rub them over the fish. Set aside for 30 minutes. Meanwhile, soak 8 bamboo skewers in water.

To make the sauce, heat the groundnut oil in a saucepan until it is nearly smoking, then turn off the heat and leave to cool completely (this preheating 'cooks' the oil and improves its flavour). Reheat the oil and add the peanuts. They should cook to a golden brown in 2–3 minutes. Transfer the peanuts and the oil to a food processor or blender and blend them to a rough paste. Add the chillies, ginger and garlic and continue to blend. Add all the remaining ingredients except the coriander and blend until smooth. Stir in the coriander and set aside.

Thread the fish pieces on to the skewers and cook on a preheated ridged grill pan (or under a hot grill) for 3–5 minutes, until cooked through, turning the skewers occasionally. Remove from the heat and serve with the peanut sauce.

600g (1 pound 5 ounces) grouper (or monkfish) fillet, skinned and cut into 2.5cm (1-inch) dice
1 tablespoon vegetable oil

For the marinade:
2 garlic cloves, peeled
1cm (½-inch) piece of fresh ginger
1 lemongrass stick, tough outer layers removed
1 teaspoon red chilli powder
1 teaspoon salt
½ teaspoon sugar
2 kaffir lime leaves, cut into fine strips
juice of 1 lemon

For the sauce:
100ml (scant ½ cup) groundnut oil
100g (1 cup) raw peanuts, skinned
2–3 Thai red chillies, chopped
1cm (½-inch) piece of fresh ginger, sliced
4 garlic cloves, peeled
100ml (scant ½ cup) fresh coconut milk
1 tablespoon Thai fish sauce
2 teaspoons dark soy sauce
1 tablespoon sugar
juice of 1 lemon
1 teaspoon salt
2 tablespoons chopped fresh coriander

PRAWNS ON TOAST

MAKES 24
or serves 6 as a starter

There are many versions of prawns on toast going around, of which the best known is probably the Chinese one, which is deep-fried. Try this great Indian spiced version for a change.

3 tablespoons vegetable or corn oil
½ teaspoon cumin seeds
I red onion, finely chopped
500g (I pound 2 ounces) raw prawns, peeled and roughly chopped
2.5cm (I-inch) piece of fresh ginger, finely chopped
2 green chillies, finely chopped
I tablespoon chopped fresh coriander
I teaspoon salt
½ teaspoon black peppercorns, crushed
150g (I¼ cups) Cheddar cheese, grated
6 slices of white bread, toasted
½ teaspoon chaat masala
juice of ½ lime

Heat the oil in a heavy-based frying pan. Add the cumin seeds, followed by the onion, and sauté until the onion is soft. Now add the prawns and stir-fry over a high heat for a couple of minutes. Add the ginger, green chillies, coriander and seasonings and mix thoroughly. Remove from the heat and leave to cool.

Stir in the cheese and spread the mixture over the toast. Flash under a hot grill for a minute, until golden brown. Cut each piece of bread into 4 squares or triangles, sprinkle the chaat masala and lime juice on top and serve immediately.

TAWA PARATHAS FILLED WITH CRAB AND PRAWN

MAKES 4

This is ideal as a between-meals snack and is very popular with children. You can also serve it as a one-dish meal; it's a good way of using up any leftover fish.

A tawa is a kind of griddle used for cooking chapattis and other breads. A heavy-based frying pan will work just as well.

To make the paratha dough, put the flour and salt in a bowl, add the oil and water and knead until it comes together into a stiff dough. Cover with a damp cloth and leave to rest for 20 minutes.

Meanwhile, make the filling. Heat the oil in a frying pan, add the cumin seeds, followed by the onion, ginger and green chillies and sauté until the onion is soft. Add the turmeric and chilli powder and sauté for a minute. Now add the prawns, sprinkle with the salt and sauté for a minute. Add the crabmeat and sauté till all the liquid evaporates. Stir in the mashed potato and mix well. Sprinkle in the coriander and squeeze the lemon over. Remove from the heat and leave to cool.

Divide the dough into 4 pieces and shape them into balls. Do the same with the filling mixture. Take a ball of dough, make an indentation in the centre and keep pressing and rotating the dough in your hand until the cavity is a little larger than the ball of stuffing. The edges of the cavity should be slightly thinner than the rest of it. Place one ball of the filling in the cavity and bring the edges of the dough together so that the filling is completely covered. Make sure there aren't any cracks or the filling will come out while you are rolling the paratha. Lightly dust with flour, gently flatten the dough with your hands, then roll out into a 15cm (6-inch) round, turning it over occasionally and making sure that the filling doesn't become exposed. Repeat with the remaining balls of dough and filling.

Heat a heavy-based frying pan, preferably cast iron, over a medium heat and place a paratha in it. Cook for 2–3 minutes, until it starts to colour underneath, then turn it over and cook the other side. Brush the top with a little of the ghee or butter, turn it over and cook until the colour has deepened. Brush the top again, turn over and repeat.

Cook the remaining parathas in the same way. Cut each paratha into quarters and serve with Curried Yoghurt with Tomatoes (see page 114).

2 tablespoons vegetable or corn oil
½ teaspoon cumin seeds
I onion, chopped
2.5cm (I-inch) piece of fresh ginger, chopped
2 green chillies, chopped
½ teaspoon ground turmeric
½ teaspoon red chilli powder
100g (4 ounces) peeled raw prawns, roughly chopped
½ teaspoon salt
100g (4 ounces) fresh white crabmeat
I large potato, boiled and mashed
I tablespoon chopped fresh coriander
juice of ½ lemon

For the paratha dough:
250g (1⅔ cups) chapatti flour
½ teaspoon salt
I tablespoon vegetable oil
125ml (½ cup) water
2 tablespoons ghee or clarified butter for brushing

STIR-FRIED KING PRAWNS WITH DRIED CHILLI, GARLIC AND SOY

SERVES 4

In this Indo-Chinese dish, the boundaries are so blurred that it's hard to say where the Indian influence ends and the Chinese one begins. One of the most popular examples of Indian-style Chinese food, it is a close cousin of the notorious 'chilli chicken'. Akin to chicken tikka masala, chilli chicken has long threatened to take over from butter chicken as the national dish of India!

Mix all the marinade ingredients together, stir in the prawns and set aside for 30 minutes.

Deep-fry the prawns in hot oil until they are golden brown, crisp and cooked through. Drain on kitchen paper and set aside.

For the stir-fry, heat the 2 tablespoons of oil in a wok until smoking. Add the dried red chillies and stir. Add the garlic and stir quickly to prevent burning, then add the diced onion and the fried prawns and stir-fry for a minute. Add the pepper and cook for another minute. Add the salt, sugar, chilli powder, ground cumin and soy and continue to stir.

When the prawns are dark and shiny, add the cornflour paste and stir quickly to mix evenly. Squeeze in the lemon juice, add the chives or spring onions and serve immediately.

12 raw king prawns, shelled and de-veined, with the tail shell left intact
oil for deep-frying
2 tablespoons vegetable or corn oil
3 dried red chillies, broken into pieces
3 garlic cloves, chopped
1 red onion, cut into 1cm (½-inch) dice
½ red or green pepper, cut into 2.5cm (1-inch) dice
1 teaspoon salt
1½ teaspoons sugar
½ teaspoon red chilli powder
1 teaspoon ground cumin
1 teaspoon dark soy sauce
1 tablespoon cornflour, mixed to a paste with a little water
juice of ½ lemon
2 tablespoons chopped chives or spring onions

For the marinade:
2 tablespoons cornflour
1 egg, lightly beaten
1 teaspoon dark soy sauce
1 tablespoon white vinegar or rice vinegar
1 garlic clove, chopped
1½ teaspoons salt

SPICED SPIDER CRAB IN FILO PASTRY WITH PLUM CHUTNEY

This is the Cinnamon Club take on a samosa, the difference being in the choice of filling. We cooked it with ordinary crabmeat several times and it was very good, but once I tried it with spider crabs from Pembroke and the texture and flavour were simply amazing. Feel free to substitute ordinary crabmeat, but if you do find spider crab believe me you will not be disappointed.

To make the chutney, heat the oil in a pan and add the onion seeds, bay leaf and dried red chillies. When they release their flavour, add the plums and cook gently until soft. Stir in the chilli powder, vinegar and sugar and simmer for 15–20 minutes, until the liquid has almost completely evaporated and the chutney is thick and glossy. Season with salt if required, then leave to cool.

You could ask your fishmonger to cook the spider crab for you, but if you are going to cook it yourself, put it in the freezer for about 2 hours first, so it becomes comatose. Then plunge it into a very large pan of boiling water and simmer for about 5 minutes. The colour of the shell will change to reddish-orange when it is cooked. Remove the crab from the pan and cool by plunging it into iced water. Drain well, then twist off the claws and legs, crack them open and remove all the meat with a fork or a pick, taking care to discard any bits of broken shell.

Open up the body shell and remove the meat, being sure to discard the gills, or 'dead man's fingers'. Heat half the ghee or clarified butter in a frying pan and add the cumin seeds. When they release their flavour, add the onion and cook, stirring until soft. Add the green chillies and ginger and sauté for a minute. Now add the crabmeat and sauté until all the liquid has evaporated. Stir in the salt, cardamom and mace. Add the chopped coriander and lemon juice, mix once and remove from the heat. Leave to cool, then divide into 12 equal portions.

Lay 3 filo pastry sheets out on a work surface and brush them with some of the remaining clarified butter. Pile them up on top of each other, then cut into 3 equal strips. Place a portion of the crab mixture towards one end of a strip and fold the filo over to make a triangle. Keep folding till you reach the other end of the pastry. Seal the end by brushing with a little beaten egg, if necessary. Repeat the process with the remaining strips of filo, then prepare the rest of the filo in the same way and fill with the rest of the crabmeat.

Place the parcels on a well-greased baking sheet, brush with the remaining clarified butter and bake in an oven preheated to 190°C/375°F/Gas Mark 5 for 8–10 minutes, until crisp and golden. Serve with the plum chutney.

SERVES 6

1 large live spider crab (or 350g (12 ounces) hand-picked fresh white crabmeat)
4 tablespoons ghee or clarified butter
1 teaspoon cumin seeds
1 large onion, chopped
4 green chillies, chopped
5cm (2-inch) piece of fresh ginger, chopped
1 teaspoon salt
½ teaspoon ground green cardamom
½ teaspoon ground mace
2 tablespoons chopped fresh coriander
juice of 1 lemon
12 filo pastry sheets (about 20cm (8 inches) square)
a little beaten egg (optional)

For the plum chutney:
2 tablespoons vegetable or corn oil
½ teaspoon black onion seeds
1 bay leaf
2 dried red chillies
500g (1 pound 2 ounces) plums, pitted and diced
1 teaspoon mild red chilli powder
3 tablespoons white vinegar
200g (7/8 cup) granulated sugar
½ teaspoon salt

CARPACCIO OF CURED WILD SALMON WITH ONION SEEDS, CUMIN, LIME AND MUSTARD OIL

RAJASTHANI SPICED SALMON SOOLA

CHARGRILLED SALMON WITH MUSTARD AND HONEY

SMOKED HADDOCK SALAD WITH LIME AND CORIANDER

SPICED SHRIMP AND POTATO CAKES

PLAICE IN CURRY LEAF AND LENTIL CRUST

TANDOORI-STYLE HALIBUT WITH GREEN SPICES

STEAMED CRAB AND COD DUMPLINGS WITH CORIANDER DIPPING SAUCE

ORISSA-STYLE STIR-FRIED SQUID

MIXED SEAFOOD 'MOILY' SOUP

TANDOORI-SPICED OYSTERS WITH PICKLED RED ONIONS

SEARED SPICE-CRUSTED SCALLOPS WITH CORIANDER MASH

STEAMED LOBSTER MOMOS WITH GINGER AND CHILLI

KERALAN LOBSTER SOUP FLAMED WITH BRANDY

STIR-FRIED SWORDFISH, FISHERMAN'S STYLE

TAWA-FRIED BLACK TIGER PRAWNS WITH CHILLI AND CORIANDER CRUST

SOFT-SHELL CRABS WITH GARLIC, CHILLI AND PEPPER

CARPACCIO OF CURED WILD SALMON WITH ONION SEEDS, CUMIN, LIME AND MUSTARD OIL

SERVES 15

This dish is a good example of how we extend the principles of Indian cooking to other ingredients. We were looking for a cold summer starter and it occurred to us that we had not tried a spiced cured salmon. We came up with this recipe, which works beautifully as a starter dressed with lime, spices and mustard oil and also as a great ingredient for an Indian-inspired salad or even a canapé, served with Curried Yoghurt (see page 114) on a piece of bread.

Although it makes quite a lot, it will keep for about 5 days in the fridge. Wild salmon is a real treat if you can get it, but otherwise look for good organic salmon.

Arrange the salmon fillets skin-side down on a baking tray and sprinkle the finely chopped lemon, lime and orange zest over them. Mix together the cumin and mustard seeds and sprinkle them over too, then cover with cling film and set aside for 2 hours.

Remove the salmon from the baking tray and set aside. Mix together the salt, sugar and red chilli powder and spread about half this mixture in a layer over the tray. Place the fillets on top, spread the chopped coriander over them and completely cover with the remaining salt mixture. Cover with cling film and leave in the fridge to cure for 8 hours. Turn the fillets over and leave for another 8 hours. Do this once more, giving a total curing time of 24 hours; the fillets should feel firm to the touch. Brush off the excess spice and salt mixture from the fillets and rinse them under cold running water, then dry on kitchen paper.

Mix together all the ingredients for the topping and sprinkle them over the flesh side of the salmon. Cover and store in the fridge.

To serve, cut the salmon into thin slices on the diagonal, lifting the slices off the skin as you go. Arrange on a plate and garnish with the lime segments and some salad leaves.

2 sides of wild salmon, weighing about 675g (1½ pounds) each
finely grated zest of 2 lemons
finely grated zest of 2 limes
finely grated zest of 1 orange
1 teaspoon cumin seeds, roasted in a dry frying pan
1 teaspoon mustard seeds, roasted in a dry frying pan
900g (2 pounds) sea salt
700g (1 pound 9 ounces) granulated sugar
3 tablespoons red chilli powder
250g (9 ounces) fresh coriander leaves and stalks, chopped

For the topping:
1 tablespoon finely chopped dill
1 tablespoon finely chopped fresh coriander
1 tablespoon red chilli powder
½ teaspoon cumin seeds
½ teaspoon mustard seeds

To garnish:
2 limes, peeled and divided into segments
a few salad leaves
2 teaspoons black onion seeds
2 teaspoons cumin seeds, roasted in a dry frying pan
2 teaspoons sea salt
mustard oil for drizzling

Sprinkle with the black onion seeds, cumin seeds, sea salt and a generous drizzle of mustard oil.

RAJASTHANI SPICED SALMON SOOLA

SERVES 4

India is renowned for its kebabs. These are the lesser-known soola kebabs, which come from princely states such as Rajasthan. The term soola refers to thinly sliced meat or fish smoked over charcoal infused with spices. It's probably best not to try this at home, so I've devised this method of heating ghee to smoking point and adding cloves to it to release their flavour. The fish is then seared in the ghee, picking up the smokiness and the flavour of the cloves beautifully.

Although boar, venison or mutton would traditionally have been used, the Rajasthani spice mix works equally well with meaty fish such as salmon, swordfish or marlin. The smokiness of cloves and the rustic spicing lend a unique earthiness to the dish.

Pat the salmon steaks dry on kitchen paper. Mix all the ingredients for the first marinade together, rub them over the fish and set aside for 15–20 minutes.

Heat the ghee or oil in a large, heavy-based frying pan and drop in the cloves. When they puff up, remove them from the pan and add the salmon. Sear over a high heat for 30 seconds on each side, then remove from the pan and leave to cool.

Now mix together all the ingredients for the second marinade and apply it to the fish. Set aside for 20 minutes, then place under a hot grill for 6–8 minutes, turning once, until well coloured. Serve with a green leafy salad.

4 x 140g (5-ounce) pieces of salmon fillet
1 tablespoon ghee or oil
4 cloves

For the first marinade:
1 teaspoon Ginger Paste (see page 12)
1 teaspoon Garlic Paste (see page 12)
1 teaspoon salt
1 teaspoon red chilli powder
1 teaspoon ground turmeric
juice of ½ lemon

For the second marinade:
1 tablespoon plain yoghurt
1 tablespoon Rajasthani Spice Paste (see page 12)
1 teaspoon chopped fresh coriander
1½ teaspoons mustard oil

CHARGRILLED SALMON WITH MUSTARD AND HONEY

SERVES 4

This dish benefits from the intense heat of a tandoor oven but also works very well at home on a barbecue. The sweet and sour elements of honey and lemon and the heat from the mustard combine exceptionally well with the rich, oily texture of salmon.

You could cook the fish in the oven instead of on a barbecue but make sure the skin crisps up.

Mix together all the ingredients for the first marinade, rub them over the fish and leave for 30 minutes.

Mix all the ingredients for the second marinade together and spread them over the fish. Leave for a further 15 minutes.

Cook the fish over a barbecue, either on skewers or directly on the grill, for 10–12 minutes, turning every 3–4 minutes. It should be crisp and well coloured. Alternatively, cook the fish on a baking tray in an oven preheated to 240°C/475°F/Gas Mark 9 (or as hot as your oven will go) for 10 minutes, then place it under a hot grill for 3 minutes on each side. Pickled Carrot, Beetroot and Radish (see page 112) makes a good accompaniment.

4 x 150g (5-ounce) pieces of salmon
    fillet

For the first marinade:
1/2 teaspoons Ginger Paste (see page 12)
1/2 teaspoons Garlic Paste (see page 12)
1½ teaspoons salt
juice of ½ lemon

For the second marinade:
100g (scant ½ cup) Greek yoghurt
2 tablespoons mustard seeds, soaked
    in 3 tablespoons white wine vinegar
    overnight and ground to a paste (or
    use 2 tablespoons wholegrain
    mustard)
½ teaspoon ground turmeric
1 teaspoon finely ground white pepper
2.5cm (1-inch) piece of fresh ginger,
    finely chopped
2 green chillies, finely chopped
1 teaspoon chopped fresh coriander
2 teaspoons chopped dill
1 tablespoon honey
2 tablespoons mustard oil
    (if unavailable, use sunflower oil)

SMOKED HADDOCK SALAD WITH LIME AND CORIANDER

SERVES 4

Serve this lovely salad as a starter or as an accompaniment to a barbecue. Try to buy the paler, undyed smoked haddock. The topping of crisp rice provides an interesting textural contrast. It is made using rice flakes, or pawa, which are available from Asian shops.

First prepare the crisp rice. Melt the ghee in a heavy-based frying pan, add the rice flakes and roast them over a low to medium heat, stirring constantly, for 4–6 minutes, until they are completely dried out and crisp but not coloured. Add the salt and pepper and roast for another 2–3 minutes, until the rice flakes turn just slightly brown and start to release a toasted aroma. Sprinkle the chaat masala over them and remove from the heat. Spread out on a baking tray and leave to cool.

Slice the smoked haddock fillet very thinly on the diagonal, lifting the slices off the skin as you go; it should look like carpaccio. Arrange the slices on a baking tray in a single layer, sprinkle with the fennel seeds and carom seeds and drizzle with the mustard oil or olive oil. Place under a very hot grill for less than a minute – just enough to warm the fillet through and glaze it lightly. Take care not to overcook it, or it will dry out. Remove from the grill, drizzle with the lime juice and leave to cool.

For the dressing, whisk together all the ingredients until emulsified. Toss the salad leaves with a tablespoon of the dressing and divide between 4 serving plates. Scatter the orange and lime segments on top, then arrange the haddock slices over the leaves and put the coriander sprigs on top of the fish. Sprinkle generously with the toasted rice flakes and serve, with the remaining dressing on the side.

1 smoked haddock fillet, weighing about 180g (6 ounces)
1 teaspoon fennel seeds
½ teaspoon carom (ajowan) seeds
1 tablespoon mustard oil or olive oil
juice of ½ lime
250g (9 ounces) mixed salad leaves
2 oranges, peeled and segmented
1 lime, peeled and segmented
8–12 sprigs of coriander

For the crisp rice:
1 tablespoon ghee
125g (4 ounces) pressed rice flakes (pawa)
a pinch of salt
½ teaspoon crushed black peppercorns
a pinch of chaat masala

For the dressing:
4 tablespoons olive oil
2 tablespoons honey
1 tablespoon lemon juice
½ teaspoon salt
1 tablespoon ginger juice, made by processing a 5cm (2-inch) piece of fresh ginger to a smooth paste, then passing it through a very fine sieve
grated zest of ½ lime

SPICED SHRIMP AND POTATO CAKES

SERVES 4

This is our version of a rather special Bengali street snack called chingri macher chop. *It has a wonderful texture and flavour and makes an excellent starter. The original dish is deep-fried but we found that shallow frying adds more texture. It is also a healthier option.*

Cook the potatoes in boiling salted water until tender, then drain and leave to cool. Peel them and grate into a bowl. Mix with the cumin seeds, ginger, green chillies and coriander. Sprinkle in the cornflour and salt and mix well. Divide the mixture into 4 and shape into balls.

To make the filling, heat the oil in a frying pan, then add the cumin seeds, followed by the onions, ginger and green chilli, and sauté for 6–8 minutes until the onions are soft. Add the turmeric and chilli powder and sauté for a minute. Now add the shrimps, sprinkle in the salt and sauté till they are well cooked. Stir in the coriander and lemon juice, then remove from the heat and leave to cool.

Take each potato ball, make an indentation in the centre with your thumb and fill it with a quarter of the shrimp mixture. Shape it back into a ball, making sure the filling is completely covered, and flatten it into a cake.

Heat the 5 tablespoons of oil in a large non-stick frying pan, add the potato cakes and fry over a low heat for 3–5 minutes on each side, until golden and crisp.

Serve with salad or Curried Yoghurt with Tomatoes (see page 114).

3 medium-sized Desiree potatoes
½ teaspoon cumin seeds, roasted in a dry frying pan
1cm (½-inch) piece of fresh ginger, finely chopped
2 green chillies, finely chopped
1 tablespoon chopped fresh coriander
1½ tablespoons cornflour
1 teaspoon salt
5 tablespoons vegetable or corn oil

For the filling:
2 tablespoons vegetable or corn oil
½ teaspoon cumin seeds
2 red onions, chopped
1cm (½-inch) piece of fresh ginger, chopped
1 green chilli, chopped
½ teaspoon ground turmeric
½ teaspoon red chilli powder
100g (4 ounces) shrimps or small prawns, coarsely chopped
½ teaspoon salt
1 tablespoon chopped fresh coriander
juice of ½ lemon

PLAICE IN CURRY LEAF AND LENTIL CRUST

SERVES 4

This really is the most amazing fried fish dish. The crisp coating of lentils and spices keeps the fish perfectly moist and provides a dramatic contrast of textures. The lentils also help retain the flavour of the marinade by preventing it coming into contact with the pan and burning. It is important to cook the fillets over a low heat with minimal movement so the crust doesn't burn. Tilapia could be used instead of plaice.

Pat the fish fillets dry on kitchen paper. Mix together all the ingredients for the marinade, rub them over the fish and set aside for 30 minutes.

To make the crust, spread the curry leaves out on a baking tray and leave in a warm place, such as the top of the oven (or in a very low oven, if you don't have the oven on), until they become dry and crisp; they should not colour at all. Crush them lightly with your hands and set aside.

Mix together the lentils, chickpeas, fennel and cumin seeds and peppercorns and gently roast them in a heavy-based frying pan until the lentils turn golden brown and the spices release their aroma. Leave to cool, then transfer to a mortar and pestle and pound to a coarse powder. Stir in the chilli flakes, curry leaves and fresh coriander.

Dust the fish fillets with the lentil and curry leaf mixture to form an even coating. You might not need all of the mixture; just use what is required to cover the fillets evenly and store the rest in an airtight container (it will keep for 2 weeks). Heat the oil in a large frying pan, add the fish fillets and fry over a low heat for about 4–5 minutes on each side. Remove and drain on kitchen paper. Serve with lemon wedges and Curried Yoghurt with Tomatoes (see page 106) or Yoghurt Rice (see page 110).

4 plaice fillets
4 tablespoons vegetable or corn oil
lemon wedges, to serve

For the marinade:

2 teaspoons salt
2 tablespoons red chilli powder
juice of ½ lemon
I teaspoon sugar
I teaspoon Ginger Paste (see page 12)
I teaspoon Garlic Paste (see page 12)

For the crust:

20 fresh curry leaves
6 tablespoons white urad lentils
I tablespoon chana dal (yellow split peas)
I teaspoon fennel seeds
½ teaspoon cumin seeds
I teaspoon black peppercorns
½ teaspoon red chilli flakes
2 tablespoons chopped fresh coriander

TANDOORI-STYLE HALIBUT WITH GREEN SPICES

I've used halibut for this dish but you could substitute salmon, swordfish or even cod to good effect. The trick is to use nice large chunks of fish – that way you can still recognise and appreciate the flavour and texture, which can be lost if the fish is overwhelmed with spices and overcooked.

You could cook this on a barbecue but you need to take care that it is not too hot – maybe even wrapping the fish in foil before placing it on the grill – otherwise the spice paste might burn.

4 x 120g (4-ounce) pieces of halibut fillet
½ teaspoon chaat masala
juice of 1 lemon

For the marinade:
1 teaspoon Ginger Paste (see page 12)
1 teaspoon Garlic Paste (see page 12)
1 teaspoon finely ground white pepper
1 teaspoon salt
½ teaspoon ground turmeric

For the green spice paste:
100g (4 ounces) fresh coriander (roots, stalks and leaves)
50g (2½ cups) mint leaves
6 green chillies, chopped
2 tablespoons vegetable or corn oil
1 teaspoon salt
½ teaspoon garam masala
3½ tablespoons Greek yoghurt

Pat the halibut fillet dry on kitchen paper. Mix together all the ingredients for the marinade, rub them over the fish and set aside for 30 minutes.

For the green spice paste, put all the ingredients except the yoghurt in a food processor or blender and process to a smooth paste. Mix the paste with the fish in a bowl, taking care not to break up the fish, then fold in the yoghurt. Leave to marinate for another 30 minutes.

Place the halibut on a baking sheet and bake for 12–15 minutes in an oven preheated to 220°C/425°F/Gas Mark 7, turning once. Remove from the oven, sprinkle with the chaat masala and lemon juice and serve.

STEAMED CRAB AND COD DUMPLINGS WITH CORIANDER DIPPING SAUCE

SERVES 4

Fresh, light and tasty, this is perfect for hot summer afternoons. It's a healthy dish, which uses very little fat. Above all, it is very simple to prepare. If you want to serve it as a main course, double the quantities and accompany with some salad.

To make the dipping sauce, pound the coriander roots, chillies and garlic to a coarse paste in a pestle and mortar or a food processor. Add the rest of the ingredients, mix well and chill.

Heat the stock with a good pinch each of the ginger, green chillies, coriander and lemongrass, then remove from the heat and set aside.

To make the dumplings, mince the cod fillet coarsely in a food processor, being careful not to blitz it to a paste, or chop it finely with a large knife. Mix it with all the rest of the ingredients, including the remaining ginger, chillies, coriander and lemongrass. Shape the mixture into small, round cakes, about 5cm (2 inches) in diameter. Transfer the dumplings to a steamer and steam for about 10 minutes, until they are cooked through. Remove from the steamer, pour the hot stock over and serve with the dipping sauce.

200ml ($^7/_8$ cup) seafood stock or fish stock
5cm (2-inch) piece of fresh ginger, finely chopped
4 green chillies, finely chopped
1 tablespoon chopped fresh coriander
1 lemongrass stalk, tough outer layers removed, finely chopped
300g (11 ounces) cod fillet, skinned
200g (7 ounces) fresh white crabmeat
25g (2 tablespoons) butter
2 red onions, finely chopped
1 teaspoon salt

For the coriander dipping sauce:
80g (3 ounces) fresh coriander roots, chopped
2 green chillies, chopped
2 red chillies, chopped
2 garlic cloves, chopped
$^1/_2$ teaspoon salt
1$^1/_2$ tablespoons palm sugar
1 tablespoon Thai fish sauce
1 tablespoon sesame oil
juice of 1 lime

ORISSA-STYLE STIR-FRIED SQUID

SERVES 4–6

We included a similar recipe to this in The Cinnamon Club Cookbook *(Absolute Press, 2003) but I've since developed it a little and added a paste of ginger and green chillies. It's my interpretation of Parsee spicing. Traditionally the same spices are used with chicken or lamb to make a type of curry but we use them to make a glaze that is then added to a quick stir-fry of squid. It works very well, as the first flavour you get is the sweetness from the apricots, followed swiftly by the heat of the ginger.*

The intensity of spices and the heat from the pan lend smokiness to this dish and the flavours are quite upfront.

For the spice paste, put the ginger and chillies in a blender or food processor with just a little water and blitz to a paste. Put the cloves, peppercorns, coriander seeds, cumin seeds and cinnamon stick on a baking sheet and place them under a hot grill for a few minutes to remove any moisture. Grind them to a powder in a spice grinder.

Heat the oil in a small pan, add the onion and sauté until golden brown. Add the garlic and sauté for a couple of minutes, then add the ginger and green chilli paste. Cook over a medium heat for 2-3 minutes, until the oil starts to separate from the mixture, then stir in the ground spices and chilli powder. Stir briskly for a few seconds, then add the tomato purée, apricot purée, salt and sugar. Cook for 3–4 minutes, until the mixture takes on a jammy consistency. It should taste sweet and spicy.

To cook the squid, heat the oil in a large, heavy-based frying pan until it starts to smoke. Add the squid rings and stir quickly until they begin to sear and colour in parts. Add the spice paste and stir-fry for a few seconds, until it coats the squid evenly. Sprinkle in the fresh coriander and squeeze over the lemon juice. Toss well, check the seasoning and serve immediately.

I tablespoon vegetable or corn oil
Ikg (2¼ pounds) squid, cleaned and cut into rings Icm (½-inch) thick
50g (I cup) fresh coriander, chopped
juice of I lemon

For the spice paste:
5cm (2-inch) piece of fresh ginger
8 green chillies
IO cloves
I teaspoon black peppercorns
½ teaspoon coriander seeds
I teaspoon cumin seeds
I cinnamon stick
2 tablespoons vegetable or corn oil
I onion, finely chopped
3 garlic cloves, finely chopped
I tablespoon red chilli powder
I tablespoon tomato purée
I tablespoon puréed semi-dried apricots
I teaspoon salt
½ teaspoon sugar

MIXED SEAFOOD 'MOILY' SOUP

SERVES 4

This is probably one of the best-known fish curries from Kerala. Brightly coloured, enriched with coconut milk and mildly spiced, yet with a pleasant sharpness from the ginger and chilli – all this makes it an immediate hit with Western palates. I've even seen some European chefs make it with pasta and dumplings! You could serve larger portions as a main course, with rice.

Heat the oil in a large frying pan, add the curry leaves, onion, ginger and green chillies and cook, stirring until the onion is soft. Add the turmeric, followed by the fish stock, coconut milk and salt, and bring to a simmer. Now add the salmon and white fish and cook for 2 minutes. Add the prawns and simmer for another 2 minutes. Finally add the squid and mussels and simmer for 2 minutes, Check the seasoning, then remove from the heat. Serve with plenty of bread.

2 tablespoons coconut or vegetable oil
20 fresh curry leaves
I large onion, sliced
2.5cm (I-inch) piece of fresh ginger, cut into thin strips
6 green chillies, slit open lengthways
½ teaspoon ground turmeric
I litre (4 cups) fish stock
400ml (I²⁄₃ cups) coconut milk
I tablespoon salt
100g (4 ounces) salmon fillet, cut into 2.5cm (I-inch) dice
100g (4 ounces) white fish fillet, such as halibut, cod or pollock, cut into 2.5cm (I-inch) dice
100g (4 ounces) shelled raw prawns
100g (4 ounces) cleaned squid, cut into rings
100g (4 ounces) fresh mussels, scrubbed and de-bearded

TANDOORI-SPICED OYSTERS WITH PICKLED RED ONIONS

SERVES 4

Oysters are, of course, wonderful served raw with just lemon and maybe that's why they are rarely seen in Indian restaurants. At the Cinnamon Club, however, we have been toying with the idea of spiced oysters for some time and, of the half a dozen or so experiments, this is the one we liked most.

Tandoori cooking is probably a touch harsh for these delicate little things but the spicing works beautifully, so I suggest marinating them with the spices and then cooking them very quickly under a hot grill. Unlike other tandoori dishes, which you can marinate for hours, or even overnight in some cases, oysters should be marinated only just before cooking, otherwise the acid in the marinade will 'cook' the oysters, giving them a rubbery texture.

First make the pickled red onions. Heat a small saucepan and dry roast the onion seeds in it for 30 seconds. Add the vinegar and water and bring to the boil, then reduce the heat and add the salt, sugar and ginger. Turn off the heat. When the liquid stops boiling, add the onions. Leave to cool, then transfer to a bowl and chill.

For the marinade, heat the vegetable or corn oil in a small pan, add the garlic and cook until golden. Stir in the gram flour and cook for 2 minutes or so, until it acquires a slightly sandy texture and releases a roasted aroma. Remove from the heat and leave to cool. Mix with all the remaining marinade ingredients to give a thick, paste-like consistency; if it is slightly runny, chill it for 15 minutes to firm it up a little.

Now coat the oysters with this marinade and arrange them either on a baking tray (if you plan to serve them in their shells) or threaded on to 8 bamboo skewers. Cook them for just a minute or so under a very hot grill. Serve immediately, in their shells or on the skewers, accompanied by the pickled red onions.

24 large oysters, shucked (you could ask your fishmonger to do this, reserving the shells for you)

For the pickled red onions:
½ teaspoon black onion seeds
2 tablespoons white wine vinegar
100ml (scant ½ cup) water
½ teaspoon salt
1 teaspoon sugar
1cm (½-inch) piece of fresh ginger, finely chopped
2 red onions, finely chopped

For the marinade:
1 tablespoon vegetable or corn oil
1 teaspoon finely chopped garlic
1 tablespoon gram flour
1 tablespoon Greek yoghurt
juice of ½ lemon
½ tablespoon chopped fresh coriander
1½ teaspoons Ginger Paste (see page 12)
1½ teaspoons Garlic Paste (see page 12)
½ teaspoon ground turmeric
2 green chillies, finely chopped
½ teaspoon salt
½ teaspoon garam masala
½ teaspoon dried fenugreek leaves, crumbled between your fingers
½ teaspoon sugar

SEARED SPICE-CRUSTED SCALLOPS WITH CORIANDER MASH

SERVES 4

Scallops are not at all common in India; they are seen only in restaurants in five-star hotels and even then not with Indian food. Most big hotels in India have as many as 4 or 5 different restaurants, each with its own separate kitchen. It was always a treat to sneak a few scallops out of the French restaurant kitchen and play about with spicing them. We tried all sorts of things, including cooking them in the tandoor, but I feel this roasted spice crust works best. It gives a fantastic crunch to the tender scallop flesh, while the lemony pan juices cut through the sweetness of the dish.

Pat the scallops dry on kitchen paper. Sprinkle the salt, black onion seeds and fennel seeds over them and set aside for a couple of minutes.

Heat the oil in a large, non-stick frying pan and sear the scallops over a medium to high heat for 1–2 minutes on each side. Remove the pan from the heat and sprinkle the coriander seeds, cumin seeds, chilli and rice flakes on top of the scallops to make an even crust. Add the butter to the pan and place the pan under a hot grill for 2 minutes, until the rice flakes turn golden brown and the butter starts foaming. Remove the scallops from the pan and mix the lemon juice into the foaming butter.

To serve, divide the Coriander Mash between 4 plates and place the scallops on top. Whisk together the pan juices and drizzle them around the scallops.

12 king scallops, the largest you can find, cleaned
I teaspoon salt
½ teaspoon black onion seeds
I teaspoon fennel seeds
I tablespoon vegetable or corn oil
I teaspoon coriander seeds, roasted in a dry frying pan and then crushed
½ teaspoon cumin seeds, roasted in a dry frying pan and then crushed
½ teaspoon red chilli flakes
I tablespoon rice flakes (pawa)
I tablespoon butter
juice of I lemon
½ quantity of Coriander Mash (see page 110)

STEAMED LOBSTER MOMOS WITH GINGER AND CHILLI

SERVES 6

I have wonderful memories of momos (Tibetan dumplings) from my time in Delhi. There were large Tibetan refugee settlements there and they had a quite separate community, with their own newspaper, restaurants, drinks and food. Momos are very popular in Delhi, even outside the Tibetan community, and are usually made with pork or chicken and occasionally seafood. This is a rather special version using lobster. Instead of making the wrappers yourself, you could use wonton wrappers, which are available from Oriental food shops.

First make the momo wrappers. Sift the flour and baking powder into a bowl. Make a well in the centre, sprinkle in the salt, then add half the water and mix well with your hands. Add the rest of the water and continue to work until the dough is smooth. Knead well for about 5 minutes. Cover and set aside for 30 minutes.

Transfer the dough to a work surface, well dusted with flour. Roll it out with your hands into a long cylindrical shape about 2.5cm (1 inch) in diameter. Cut into pieces 2.5cm (1 inch) long, then dust each piece with flour and flatten into a round. Using a rolling pin, roll out each piece into a circle about 7.5–8cm (3–3½ inches) in diameter and the thickness of a 10-pence coin. Stack the circles up as you go, dusting with cornflour between each layer and covering them with a damp cloth to prevent them drying out.

To make the filling, twist off the claws from the lobsters, crack them open and remove all the meat. Remove the meat from the body. Chop the lobster meat roughly and mix with all the other ingredients. Take a momo wrapper, brush the edge with water and place a heaped teaspoonful of the filling in the centre. Pull up the edges around the filling and make small folds all the way round to pleat them. Now hold all the folds together and twist them slightly to seal the opening. Repeat with the remaining wrappers and filling.

Transfer the momos to a steamer (you will probably have to cook them in 2 or 3 batches) and steam for about 10–12 minutes, until the filling is cooked through. If you are using wonton pastry they will take only 6–8 minutes. Serve with the Chilli and Garlic Dip.

2 live lobsters, cut in half lengthways and cleaned (you can ask your fishmonger to do this, as long as you cook the lobsters on the same day)
1 red onion, chopped
2 garlic cloves, chopped
5cm (2-inch) piece of fresh ginger, chopped
4 green chillies, chopped
2 spring onions, chopped
1 teaspoon black peppercorns, crushed
2 tablespoons chopped fresh coriander
1 lemongrass stick, tough outer layers removed, finely chopped
50g (3½ tablespoons) butter
1½ teaspoons salt
juice of 1 lemon
Chilli and Garlic Dip (see page 115), to serve

For the wrappers:
200g (1⅓ cups) plain flour
½ teaspoon baking powder
a good pinch of salt
100ml (scant ½ cup) water
3 tablespoons cornflour for dusting

KERALAN LOBSTER SOUP FLAMED WITH BRANDY

SERVES 4

This is a great soup, the Indian equivalent of the famous lobster bisque, except that there is no rice for thickening. Instead the soup is thickened by an emulsion of coconut milk and cream. It has proved very popular at the Cinnamon Club and has made numerous appearances on our menu.

Twist off the claws from the lobsters, crack them open and remove all the meat. Remove the meat from the body, then cut all the meat into 1cm (½-inch) cubes, reserving the trimmings and the shells.

To make the stock, put all the ingredients in a large pan and bring to the boil. Reduce the heat and simmer for 20 minutes, then strain through a fine sieve and set aside.

To make the spice mix, pound all the ingredients together to a coarse paste in a mortar and pestle.

Heat the oil and half the butter in a saucepan, add the spice mix and curry leaves and sauté until the garlic turns golden brown. Add the chilli powder and the lobster trimmings and sauté for a minute. Add the tomatoes and salt and stir till the tomatoes soften. Now add the stock and bring to a simmer. Reduce the heat and cook gently for 30 minutes. Remove from the heat and leave to cool. Blend the soup with a hand blender and pass it through a fine sieve.

Heat the remaining butter in a large saucepan, add the lobster meat and sauté for a minute. Pour the soup into the pan and bring to a simmer. Stir in the coconut milk, cream, sugar, lemon juice and coriander, then remove from the heat. Pour the brandy into a ladle and warm it over a low flame until it catches fire. Pour the brandy over the soup, cover and leave to stand for 2 minutes. Divide the soup and lobster meat between 4 soup plates and serve straight away.

2 live lobsters, cut in half lengthways and cleaned (you can ask your fishmonger to do this, as long as you cook the lobsters on the same day)
1 tablespoon vegetable or corn oil
25g (2 tablespoons) butter
10 fresh curry leaves
½ teaspoon red chilli powder
3 ripe tomatoes, quartered
1 teaspoon salt
2 tablespoons coconut milk
1 tablespoon single cream
½ teaspoon sugar
juice of 1 lemon
1 tablespoon chopped fresh coriander
1 tablespoon brandy

For the stock:
the shells from the lobsters
200g (7 ounces) prawn shells (optional)
1 litre (4 cups) water
1 onion, diced
½ carrot, diced
½ celery stalk, diced
3 shiitake mushrooms, cut in half
3 bay leaves
1½ teaspoons coriander seeds
1 teaspoon black peppercorns
50g (2 ounces) fresh coriander roots
1 teaspoon salt

For the spice mix:
2 garlic cloves, peeled
1 tablespoon coriander seeds
1 teaspoon cumin seeds
1 teaspoon black peppercorns

STIR-FRIED SWORDFISH, FISHERMAN'S STYLE

SERVES 4

Back in India, this would be made with kingfish or another large fish such as bekti but it is just as good with any firm, meaty fish. I think it works beautifully with swordfish. Serve with salad and Curried Yoghurt with Tomatoes (see page 114) – plus, if you like, Squid Ink and Sesame Naan (see page 116).

600g (I pound 5 ounces) swordfish, cut
    into 2.5cm (I-inch) dice
oil for deep-frying
2 teaspoons vegetable or corn oil
I red onion, chopped
2.5cm (I-inch) piece of fresh ginger,
    finely chopped
4 green chillies, cut lengthways in half
I teaspoon red chilli powder
2 tablespoons chopped mint
I tablespoon chopped fresh coriander
I teaspoon salt
2 tablespoons tamarind chutney or
    tamarind paste
juice of ½ lemon

For the batter:
I tablespoon jaggery or molasses sugar
6 tablespoons water
4 tablespoons rice flour
2 teaspoons mild red chilli powder
I teaspoon salt
I tablespoon tamarind paste

To make the batter, dissolve the jaggery or molasses in the water, then mix with all the rest of the ingredients until smooth. Coat the swordfish pieces in the batter and deep-fry in hot oil for 2 minutes, until the batter is crisp but the fish is still succulent. Drain on kitchen paper and set aside.

Heat the 2 teaspoons of oil in a wok or large frying pan, add the onion and sauté till golden brown. Add the ginger, green chillies and red chilli powder, then the swordfish, and stir quickly to mix everything together well. Add the mint, coriander and salt and stir till the herbs have wilted. Now stir in the tamarind chutney or paste until you get a glaze on the fish. Squeeze in the lemon juice and serve immediately.

TAWA-FRIED BLACK TIGER PRAWNS WITH CHILLI AND CORIANDER CRUST

SERVES 4

Black tiger prawns are a seawater variety and have a firm texture compared to freshwater prawns, which are sweeter and more juicy. They are quite good for grilling and this dish could just as easily be cooked on a barbecue. It is ideal for a light summer lunch.

If you don't have a tawa to cook the prawns in, a flat griddle or heavy-based frying pan will do just as well.

Using kitchen scissors, slit the king prawns open along the back, taking care to leave the shell attached. Remove the black intestinal vein with the tip of a knife, then open the prawns out flat to 'butterfly' them. Pat the prawns dry on kitchen paper to get rid of excess moisture.

Mix together the salt and spices and sprinkle half this mixture evenly over the exposed flesh of the opened prawns. Spread the oil over a preheated flat griddle or heavy-based frying pan and place the prawns on it, flesh-side down. Cook the prawns for 3–4 minutes over a medium heat until lightly coloured, pressing them down lightly if they start to curl away.

Remove the prawns from the heat, brush with the clarified butter and sprinkle the remaining spice mix on top. Place them under a hot grill for a minute or two, until the spices start to release their aroma. Remove, sprinkle with the chives and squeeze the lemon juice on top. Serve immediately, with a green leafy salad.

500g (1 pound 2 ounces) raw black
    tiger prawns, heads removed
1 tablespoon salt
1 tablespoon dried red chilli flakes
1 tablespoon cumin seeds, crushed
1 tablespoon coriander seeds, crushed
1 tablespoon vegetable or corn oil
2 tablespoons ghee or clarified butter
1 tablespoon chopped fresh chives
juice of 1 lemon

SOFT-SHELL CRABS WITH GARLIC, CHILLI AND PEPPER

SERVES 6

If you can find soft-shell crabs, it's definitely worth trying this simple but delicious recipe. You may only be able to obtain frozen ones, in which case you will have to thaw them before use.

You might have some batter left over after frying the crabs. If so, you could fry a small batch of sprats or whitebait in it – wonderful with pre-dinner drinks.

Mix together all the ingredients for the marinade and rub them over the crab. Set aside in the refrigerator for 15 minutes.

For the batter, put all the dry ingredients in a bowl and slowly whisk in the vinegar and sparkling water to make a thick, smooth mixture the consistency of pancake batter. Coat the marinated crab in the batter and shake off the excess. Deep-fry in hot oil for 3–4 minutes, until crisp. Drain on kitchen paper and serve immediately, with a salad of your choice.

6 soft-shell crabs, thawed if frozen, then washed and patted dry
oil for deep-frying

For the marinade:
1 teaspoon Ginger Paste (see page 12)
1 teaspoon Garlic Paste (see page 12)
1 teaspoon red chilli powder
1 tablespoon lemon juice
1 teaspoon salt

For the batter:
5 tablespoons cornflour
100g (½ cup) rice flour
4 teaspoons red chilli powder
2 teaspoons salt
2 teaspoons black peppercorns, crushed
5 garlic cloves, finely chopped
a sprig of fresh curry leaves, shredded
50ml (3½ tablespoons) white vinegar
180ml (¾ cup) sparkling water

SEARED HALIBUT IN MALABAR CURRY SAUCE TURBOT WITH
GOAN CURRY SAUCE LEMON SOLE ROLLED WITH SPICED
PRAWNS, GREEN SPICED SAUCE SEARED COD WITH LIME
LEAF AND TOMATO SAUCE COD BAKED IN AN ENVELOPE
SPICE-CRUSTED SEA BREAM WRAPPED IN BANANA LEAF
WITH GREEN MANGO AND COCONUT CHUTNEY POPPY SEED
CRUSTED HOT AND SWEET TILAPIA WITH YOGHURT SAUCE
MULLET OR MACKEREL CALDEEN RED SNAPPER WITH
GINGER-JAGGERY CHUTNEY ROASTED WHOLE MACKEREL
WITH LEMONGRASS AND SPICES SPICE-CRUSTED WHOLE
FISH CUMIN- AND CHILLI-CRUSTED SALMON STEAKS
WITH GOAN XACUTI SAUCE KEDGEREE WITH POACHED EGG
AND SMOKED HADDOCK SEMOLINA-CRUSTED SEA BASS
WITH CASHEW NUT SAUCE PERCH IN RAJASTHANI YOGHURT
SOUP BLACK COD AND CRAB KOFTA WITH KERALA CURRY
SAUCE SEARED SCALLOPS WITH TAMARIND AND CHILLI
MUNG BEAN KEDGEREE KERALA-STYLE BIRYANI WITH
MUSSELS AND MONKFISH WILD PRAWNS SIMMERED IN CHILLI
TOMATO AND LIME SAUCE SEAFOOD 'KHICHRI'
TANDOORI-STYLE KING PRAWNS WITH FENNEL AND
CORIANDER SEEDS KING CRAB CLAWS WITH GARLIC AND
PEPPER BUTTER

SEARED HALIBUT IN MALABAR CURRY SAUCE

SERVES 4

4 x 200g (7-ounce) pieces of halibut fillet
½ teaspoon ground turmeric
I teaspoon salt
2 tablespoons ghee or clarified butter

For the spice crust:
I teaspoon allspice berries
½ nutmeg
I teaspoon black peppercorns
2 blades of mace
5cm (2-inch) piece of cinnamon stick
6 green cardamom pods
5cm (2-inch) piece of dried ginger

Spice mix for the sauce:
3 tablespoons coriander seeds
½ teaspoon fenugreek seeds
2 green cardamom pods
2.5cm (I-inch) piece of cinnamon stick
2 cloves
2 bay leaves
2 teaspoons fennel seeds
I star anise
I teaspoon cumin seeds

For the Malabar curry sauce:
3 tablespoons coconut or vegetable oil
5cm (2-inch) piece of cinnamon stick
4 green cardamom pods

4 cloves
I bay leaf
½ teaspoon mustard seeds
IO fresh curry leaves
2 onions, chopped
5cm (2-inch) piece of fresh ginger, cut
    into thin strips
4 green chillies, cut lengthways in half
½ teaspoon ground turmeric
I teaspoon red chilli powder
I tomato, chopped
I teaspoon salt
IOOml (scant ½ cup) coconut milk
I tablespoon tamarind paste
I tablespoon chopped fresh coriander

Halibut is rarely used in traditional Indian kitchens but its meaty texture works very well in a tandoor oven. Here it is seared in a pan with a spice coating and then cooked quite slowly like a French confit, to give a nice crust and a succulent interior.

Pat the halibut dry on kitchen paper, rub with the turmeric and salt and set aside for 30 minutes.

To make the spice crust, roast all the ingredients in a dry, heavy-based frying pan for 3–5 minutes, until they become pleasantly fragrant. Leave to cool, then grind to a coarse powder in a mortar and pestle. Dust the fish pieces with this mixture and set aside.

To make the spice mix for the sauce, roast all the ingredients in the same way as for the spice crust and then grind to a fine powder in a food processor or spice grinder.

To make the sauce, heat the oil in a large frying pan and add the cinnamon, cardamom, cloves, bay leaf and mustard seeds. When the mustard seeds begin to crackle, add the curry leaves and onions and cook, stirring, until the onions are soft but not coloured. Add the ginger and green chillies, followed by the turmeric, chilli powder and a tablespoon of the spice mix (the remainder can be stored in an airtight container for 3 weeks). Stir for a minute, then add the tomato and salt and cook till the tomato is soft. Add the coconut milk and tamarind paste and simmer for 2–3 minutes. Sprinkle in the coriander and remove from the heat.

To cook the fish, heat the ghee or clarified butter in a heavy-based frying pan, add the halibut and cook over a low to medium heat for about 5 minutes on each side, spooning the fat over the fish all the time. Remove from the heat and serve with the sauce. Accompany with simple, plain rice.

TURBOT WITH GOAN CURRY SAUCE

SERVES 4

This recipe combines Goan and Keralan spicing with European cooking techniques and the results are stunning. Although easy to prepare it looks very impressive, and does not shy away from upfront flavours. The layers of flavour and texture help to highlight the quality of a prime fish like turbot.

For the spice mix, dry roast the spices individually in a frying pan over a low heat until they release their aroma. Blend them with the garlic and vinegar in a food processor or a pestle and mortar, gradually adding the sugar and salt.

For the sauce, heat the oil in a deep pan, add the onion and sauté until it is soft and starting to turn light golden. Add the chilli powder and cook for 30 seconds. Add the tomatoes and cook for 4–6 minutes, until they have disintegrated and are almost dry. Now lower the heat, add the spice mix and cook for 5–6 minutes, until the oil starts to separate from the mixture. Add the fish stock and simmer for 3–4 minutes. Raise the heat, add the coconut milk and simmer for about 5 minutes, till the sauce thickens and becomes glossy. It should taste hot and sour.

Rub the salt and turmeric over the fish, sprinkle the onion seeds and curry leaves on top and set aside for 10 minutes. Heat the oil in a heavy-based frying pan, add the fish, skin-side down, and sear for 2 minutes, until the skin is crisp. Turn over, reduce the heat and cook for 3 minutes longer. Transfer the fish to 4 serving plates and pour the sauce around. Serve with Spinach Tempered with Cumin and Garlic (see page 111).

1 teaspoon salt
1 teaspoon ground turmeric
8 x 100g (3½-ounce) pieces of turbot
    fillet
10 fresh curry leaves, coarsely chopped
½ teaspoon black onion seeds
1½ tablespoons vegetable or corn oil

For the Goan spice mix:
10 cloves
1 tablespoon coriander seeds
1½ teaspoons black peppercorns
2 black cardamom pods
3 star anise
5 dried red chillies
4 garlic cloves, chopped
2 tablespoons white vinegar
1 tablespoon sugar
1 teaspoon salt

For the Goan curry sauce:
50ml (3½ tablespoons) vegetable or
    corn oil
1 onion, finely chopped
½ teaspoon red chilli powder
2 tomatoes, chopped
125ml (½ cup) fish stock
100ml (scant ½ cup) coconut milk

LEMON SOLE ROLLED WITH SPICED PRAWNS, GREEN SPICED SAUCE

SERVES 4

Here is another example of a dish that combines Indian spicing with European cooking techniques and presentation. Sole is quite a pliable fish and so is particularly good for this recipe; you could try plaice as an alternative.

This recipe is ideal for a dinner party. You could prepare the skewers and sauce in advance and just take a few minutes to assemble the dish in full view of your audience!

Pat the fish fillets and prawns dry on kitchen paper. Rub the turmeric, onion seeds and half the salt over the fish and set aside for 15 minutes.

Heat a tablespoon of the oil in a frying pan, add the prawns and sauté for 30 seconds, until they turn pink. Mix in the chilli powder and the remaining salt and leave to cool.

Bring a large saucepan of water to the boil, add the spinach and stir it around in the water for 30 seconds, until just wilted. Drain well, refresh in a bowl of ice-cold water, then drain again and dry on kitchen paper.

Lay one of the fish fillets out on a work surface and arrange some of the spinach leaves on top to cover it. Sprinkle with garam masala and place

half a prawn at the tail end of the fillet, then roll it up towards the head end. Secure with a bamboo skewer and repeat with the rest of the fillets.

To prepare the sauce, heat the oil in a frying pan, add the onion, ginger, garlic and green chillies and sauté till the onion is soft. Add the cashew nuts and sauté until they turn golden. Add the coriander and mint and sauté again until softened. Remove from the heat and leave to cool, then blend to a smooth paste in a blender or food processor, adding a little water if required.

For the tempering, heat the oil in a frying pan and add the mustard seeds and red chillies. When the mustard seeds crackle and the chillies change colour, add the sauce and bring to the boil. Season with the salt and sugar, add the lemon juice, then remove from the heat and keep warm.

To cook the fish, heat the remaining 3 tablespoons of oil in a large, non-stick frying pan, add the rolled-up fillets and fry them on all sides for a couple of minutes. Transfer them to a baking tray, dot the butter over the top and bake in an oven preheated to 180°C/350°F/Gas Mark 4 for 4–6 minutes. To serve, spoon a couple of tablespoons of the sauce on to each plate and place 2 rolls on top.

8 x 175g (6-ounce) lemon sole fillets, skinned and cut lengthways in half
4 raw, headless king prawns, peeled, de-veined and cut lengthways in half
½ teaspoon ground turmeric
½ teaspoon black onion seeds
I teaspoon salt
4 tablespoons vegetable or corn oil
½ teaspoon red chilli powder
10–12 large spinach leaves
I teaspoon garam masala
I tablespoon butter

For the green spiced sauce:
2 tablespoons vegetable or corn oil
I onion, sliced
5cm (2-inch) piece of fresh ginger, roughly chopped
6 garlic cloves, roughly chopped
4 green chillies, roughly chopped
50g (½ cup) broken unsalted cashew nuts
150g (2½ cups) fresh coriander, roughly chopped
50g (2 cups) mint, roughly chopped

For the tempering:
I tablespoon vegetable or corn oil
½ teaspoon mustard seeds
2–3 dried red chillies
I teaspoon salt
½ teaspoon sugar
juice of I lemon

SEARED COD WITH LIME LEAF AND TOMATO SAUCE

4 x 200g (7-ounce) pieces of cod (or
    pollock) fillet
1½ tablespoons vegetable or corn oil
1½ teaspoons salt
½ teaspoon black onion seeds
1 teaspoon fennel seeds
15g (1 tablespoon) butter

For the spice mix:
½ teaspoon coriander seeds
½ teaspoon cumin seeds
½ teaspoon black peppercorns
1 dried red chilli
1 fresh lime leaf

For the lime leaf and tomato sauce:
3 tablespoons ghee or clarified butter
1 bay leaf
6 ripe tomatoes, boiled in a little water
    until tender, then pushed through a
    sieve to make a purée
1 teaspoon Ginger Paste (see page 12)
1 teaspoon Garlic Paste (see page 12)
1 teaspoon red chilli powder
1 teaspoon ground cumin
300ml (1½ cups) coconut milk
1½ teaspoons salt
½ teaspoon sugar
2 fresh lime leaves
1 lemongrass stick, lightly crushed

For the garnish:
½ tablespoon vegetable or corn oil
½ red pepper, cut into fine matchsticks
½ green pepper, cut into fine
    matchsticks
1 red onion, thinly sliced
1 small green mango, peeled, pitted and
    cut into fine matchsticks (optional)
a pinch of salt
a pinch of sugar
juice of ½ lime

SERVES 4

This is a modern Indian dish with several different components, each contributing towards the texture, flavour and appearance. It's surprisingly straightforward to prepare.

Wash the cod fillets and pat them dry on kitchen paper. Mix ½ tablespoon of the oil with the salt, onion seeds and fennel seeds. Rub this mixture over the fish and set aside for 15 minutes.

For the spice mix, lightly roast all the ingredients in a dry frying pan or in a very low oven, then pound them coarsely in a mortar and pestle.

For the sauce, heat the ghee or butter in a pan, add the bay leaf and sieved tomatoes and simmer for 5 minutes.

In a bowl, mix the ginger and garlic pastes, chilli powder and cumin with a little water to make a smooth paste. Add this mixture to the pan and simmer for 5 minutes, stirring to prevent sticking. Sprinkle in the spice mix, stir in the coconut milk and simmer for 3–4 minutes, until the sauce turns glossy. Now add the salt, sugar, lime leaves and lemongrass. Simmer for another 3–4 minutes, until the sauce is infused with the lemon and lime flavours.

To cook the fish, heat the remaining oil in a large, ovenproof frying pan, add the fish and sear for 2–3 minutes on each side. Add the butter, transfer the pan to an oven preheated to 180°C/350°F/Gas Mark 4 and cook for 8–10 minutes, until the fish is done. Remove the fish from the oven, drain it on a kitchen cloth and keep warm.

For the garnish, heat the oil in a pan, add the peppers and onion and stir-fry quickly over a high heat for just under a minute. Add the green mango, if using, and the salt and sugar and mix through; the vegetables should still be crunchy. Remove from the heat immediately.

To serve, place the cod on 4 plates and pour the sauce around. Garnish with the stir-fried vegetables. Spinach and Coconut Porial (see page 113) makes a good accompaniment.

COD BAKED IN AN ENVELOPE

SERVES 4

I have fond memories of this dish; it was my first bestseller some 10 years ago in the Oberoi Grand Hotel in Calcutta. Then I used to use Calcutta bekti but cod, or even perch, makes a good alternative. It's a simple, healthy dish with a beautiful flavour.

Mix together all the ingredients for the marinade and use to coat the cod. Set aside for 15 minutes.

Meanwhile, prepare the vegetables. Mix the butter with the sliced potatoes, nutmeg and half the salt and set aside. Mix the rest of the vegetables with lemon, thyme, sugar, garlic and the remaining salt and set aside for 10 minutes.

Cut 4 pieces of baking parchment, about 30cm (12 inches) square. Place the potatoes slices on the paper, slightly off centre, then place the vegetables on top of the potatoes, fishing out a lemon slice to place on each mound. Place the marinated cod on top of the lemon slices. Now fold over the paper to cover the fish and crimp the edges to seal the parcels completely. Place on a greased baking tray and bake in an oven preheated to 180°C/350°F/Gas Mark 4 for 12–15 minutes.

Remove from the oven, cut open the envelopes with scissors (take care, as the escaping steam can cause burns) and transfer the contents to 4 serving plates. Serve immediately, pouring the cooking juices over the fish. Accompany with Coriander Mash (see page 110).

4 x 200g (7-ounce) pieces of cod fillet, skinned

For the marinade:
I teaspoon salt
juice of ½ lemon
I½ teapoons Ginger Paste (see page 12)
I½ teapoons Garlic Paste (see page 12)
I tablespoon mustard oil
I tablespoon ghee or clarified butter
2 tablespoons kasundi mustard or Dijon mustard
I tablespoon chopped dill

For the vegetables:
½ tablespoon butter
2 potatoes, peeled and thinly sliced on a mandoline or with the slicing attachment of a food processor
⅛ nutmeg, grated
I teaspoon salt
I celery stalk, cut into 3cm x 5mm (I¼ x ¼ inch) batons
½ red pepper cut into 3cm x 5mm (I¼ x ¼ inch) batons
I red onion, sliced 5mm (¼ inch) thick
4 shiitake mushrooms, stalks removed, cut into slices 5mm (¼ inch) thick
½ fennel bulb, cut into slices 5mm (¼ inch) thick
I lemon, cut into slices 5mm (¼ inch) thick
I sprig of thyme
½ teaspoon sugar
½ teaspoon chopped garlic

SPICE-CRUSTED SEA BREAM WRAPPED IN BANANA LEAF WITH GREEN MANGO AND COCONUT CHUTNEY

SERVES 4

Coating fish with an intense spice mix and cooking it in banana leaves is a traditional technique from Kerala. The leaves protect the spices from burning and seal the flavours inside, keeping the fish moist. The charred leaves are then discarded before serving. Banana leaves are available from some Indian, Thai and Caribbean food shops. If you can't get hold of them, put the fish in a hot pan to caramelise it underneath, then cover the pan with foil, making sure it doesn't touch the fish, and finish the cooking.

Sprinkle the sea bream fillets with the red chilli powder, salt and lime juice and set aside to marinate for 30 minutes.

For the spice crust, pound the shallots, garlic and peppercorns to a coarse paste in a pestle and mortar. Add the rest of the ingredients and mix well.

Heat the banana leaves in a hot frying pan until they are soft and pliable (or heat them in a microwave for about 30 seconds). Cover the bream fillets on both sides with the spice crust, wrap each one in a banana leaf, then set aside.

For the chutney, put all the ingredients in a food processor and blend to a smooth paste, adding a little more water if required.

To cook the fish, heat the tablespoon of oil in a heavy-based frying pan. Place the wrapped-up bream fillets in the pan, then cover and cook over a low heat for 3–5 minutes on each side. Remove the leaves and serve the bream with the chutney.

4 x 150g (5-ounce) sea bream fillets, scaled and pin-boned
½ teaspoon red chilli powder
½ teaspoon salt
juice of ½ lime
4 banana leaves, cut into 25–30cm (10–12-inch) squares
1 tablespoon vegetable or corn oil

For the spice crust:
5 shallots, peeled
4 garlic cloves, peeled
20 black peppercorns
1 teaspoon red chilli powder
20 curry leaves, finely shredded
2 tablespoons vegetable or corn oil
1½ teaspoons salt
1 teaspoon sugar
3 tablespoons white vinegar

For the green mango and coconut chutney:
3 green mangoes, peeled, pitted and diced
80g (1 cup) grated fresh coconut
1 shallot, sliced
1 garlic clove, peeled
2 teaspoons red chilli powder
1 tablespoon vegetable or corn oil
1 teaspoon salt
½ teaspoon sugar
3 tablespoons water

POPPY SEED CRUSTED HOT AND SWEET TILAPIA WITH YOGHURT SAUCE

SERVES 4

The hot and sweet elements in this dish contrast with the freshness of the yoghurt sauce, while poppy seeds add an extra dimension to the texture. You could use sea bass instead of tilapia.

Pat the fish fillets dry on kitchen paper. Mix together all the ingredients for the marinade, rub them over the fish and set aside for 30 minutes. Meanwhile, roast the poppy seeds in a dry frying pan until golden, then set aside.

To make the sauce, heat the oil in a heavy-based pan, add the onion and sauté till golden brown. Stir in the cashew paste and cook over a low heat, stirring constantly, until the oil separates out from the mixture. Add the turmeric and sauté for a minute. Add the yoghurt and cook over a moderate heat for 2 minutes.

Add the fish stock and cook for another 3 minutes. Now add the ginger, salt and sugar and simmer until the oil starts to separate from the sauce around the edge of the pan. Stir in the lemon juice and fresh coriander, then set aside and keep warm.

Place the fish fillets on a non-stick baking sheet and drizzle with the oil. Cook for 4–6 minutes in an oven preheated to 200°C/400°F/Gas Mark 6. Remove from the oven, sprinkle with the toasted poppy seeds and place under a hot grill for 3–4 minutes, taking care that the poppy seeds do not burn.

Divide the sauce between 4 serving plates, put the fish on top and serve with plain rice on the side.

8 tilapia fillets
3 tablespoons white poppy seeds
2 tablespoons vegetable or corn oil

For the marinade:
2 tablespoons red chilli powder
1 teaspoon Ginger Paste (see page 12)
1 teaspoon Garlic Paste (see page 12)
1½ teaspoons salt
1 tablespoon jaggery or molasses sugar
juice of 2 lemons

For the yoghurt sauce:
3 tablespoons vegetable or corn oil
1 onion, finely chopped
100g (½ cup) Boiled Cashew Paste
   (see page 12)
1 teaspoon ground turmeric
200g (⅞ cup) plain yoghurt
4 tablespoons fish stock
2.5cm (1-inch) piece of fresh ginger,
   finely chopped
1 teaspoon salt
½ teaspoon sugar
juice of ½ lemon
1 tablespoon chopped fresh coriander

MULLET OR MACKEREL CALDEEN

SERVES 4

This is the Cinnamon Club version of what is otherwise a traditional Goan fish preparation. It can be served either with the cooked fish on top of the sauce or by tossing the fish in the sauce at the last minute.

Pat the fish fillets dry on kitchen paper. Mix together all the ingredients for the marinade and rub them over the fish. Set aside for 30 minutes.

To make the sauce, heat the oil in a frying pan, add the onion and sauté till soft. Add the garlic, ginger and green chillies, followed by the ground spices, and sauté for a minute. Add the coconut milk and water or fish stock and simmer for 5 minutes. Stir in the salt, vinegar and coriander, then check the seasoning. Add the sugar if you feel it is too sour. Remove from the heat and set aside.

To cook the fish, heat the 2 tablespoons of oil in a large frying pan, add the fish fillets and fry for about 2 minutes on each side. Serve with the sauce and some plain rice.

8 red mullet or mackerel fillets, scaled and pin boned
2 tablespoons vegetable or corn oil

For the marinade:
1 teaspoon salt
1 teaspoon ground turmeric
1 teaspoon Ginger Paste (see page 12)
1 teaspoon Garlic Paste (see page 12)

For the sauce:
2 tablespoons vegetable or corn oil
1 large onion, sliced
2 garlic cloves, chopped
2.5cm (1-inch) piece of fresh ginger, chopped
4 green chillies, slit lengthways in half
½ teaspoon ground turmeric
1 teaspoon ground cumin seeds
1 tablespoon ground coriander seeds
1 teaspoon black peppercorns, crushed
250ml (1 cup) coconut milk
100ml (scant ½ cup) water or fish stock
1 teaspoon salt
2 tablespoons white vinegar
1 tablespoon chopped fresh coriander
½ teaspoon sugar (optional)

RED SNAPPER WITH GINGER–JAGGERY CHUTNEY

SERVES 4

This is a very simple recipe, ideal for entertaining. The chutney can be prepared in advance, just leaving you to cook the fish. The combination of intense ginger chutney with fish is strikingly unusual and makes a pleasing change from a more liquid sauce. Serve with Mustard Mash (see page 111).

Pat the snapper fillets dry on kitchen paper. Mix together the salt, chilli powder, black onion seeds, carom seeds and a tablespoon of the oil and rub them over the fish, then set aside.

To make the chutney, heat the oil in a frying pan, add the sliced ginger and fry until golden brown and crisp. Remove the ginger with a slotted spoon and leave to cool, then pound to a coarse paste. Reheat the oil in the pan and add the mustard and fenugreek seeds. When they begin to crackle, add the green chillies and curry leaves. Then add the ground ginger and red chilli powder and stir till the oil separates from the mixture. Add the tamarind, jaggery and salt and cook for about 30 minutes, until the oil is floating on top of the chutney. Remove from the heat and leave to cool.

To cook the fish, heat the remaining 2 tablespoons of oil in a large frying pan, add the fish fillets, skin-side down, and fry over a low heat for 4–5 minutes on each side. Serve immediately, with the chutney.

8 red snapper fillets, cleaned and cut in half
2 teaspoons salt
½ teaspoon red chilli powder
I teaspoon black onion seeds
½ teaspoon carom (ajowan) seeds
3 tablespoons vegetable or corn oil

For the ginger–jaggery chutney:
3 tablespoons vegetable or corn oil
7.5cm (3-inch) piece of fresh ginger, thinly sliced
½ teaspoon mustard seeds
½ teaspoon fenugreek seeds
2 green chillies, cut lengthwise in half
5 fresh curry leaves
½ teaspoon red chilli powder
I tablespoon tamarind paste
I½ tablespoons jaggery or molasses sugar, dissolved in 3 tablespoons water
I teaspoon salt

ROASTED WHOLE MACKEREL WITH LEMONGRASS AND SPICES

SERVES 4

This is one of the easiest recipes in the book. Pick really long stalks of lemongrass and let some of the stalk stick out of the fishes' mouths; it looks really dramatic. Another way of cooking this would be to wrap the fish in banana leaves, cook them on a hot pan or barbecue for a few minutes on either side and then finish in the oven if necessary.

Slash the mackerel 2 or 3 times on each side with a sharp knife. Rub in the salt and chilli powder and set aside for 30 minutes.

Make the spice paste by blending all the ingredients together in a food processor or blender. Cover both sides of each fish with the spice paste, insert a stalk of lemongrass through the mouth and set aside for another 30 minutes.

Place the fish on a baking tray and cook in an oven preheated to 180°C/350°F/Gas Mark 4 for 12–15 minutes, turning them over once half way through the cooking time. Serve with the lemon wedges.

4 mackerel, cleaned and fins trimmed
2 teaspoons salt
2 teaspoons red chilli powder
4 lemongrass stalks, bruised
lemon wedges, to serve

For the spice paste:
8 shallots, peeled
2 garlic cloves, peeled
2.5cm (I-inch) piece of fresh ginger
I teaspoon ground turmeric
5 dried red chillies, soaked in warm
    water for 30 minutes, then drained
2 green chillies
I teaspoon fennel seeds
I teaspoon mustard seeds
IO fresh curry leaves
I tablespoon tamarind paste
2 tablespoons vegetable or corn oil
I teaspoon salt
½ teaspoon sugar

SPICE-CRUSTED WHOLE FISH

SERVES 4

A wide variety of fish are suitable for this recipe, as long as they're the right size to serve one per person. The firm texture of snapper in particular makes it ideal for roasting and works really well with the flavours of the spices.

4 x 350–400g (12–14-ounce) whole fish, such as snapper, bass or bream, cleaned and fins and tail trimmed
4 tablespoons ghee or clarified butter
lemon wedges, to serve

For the marinade:
2 tablespoons salt
4 tablespoons red chilli powder
2 teaspoons ground turmeric
juice of 4 lemons

For the spice crust:
6 tablespoons coriander seeds
5 tablespoons cumin seeds
4 teaspoons black peppercorns
250g (9 ounces) fresh coriander, chopped
12 garlic cloves, peeled
5cm (2-inch) piece of fresh ginger, chopped
1 tablespoon red chilli powder
1 tablespoon salt
2 teaspoons sugar
4 tablespoons vegetable or corn oil

Mix together all the ingredients for the marinade. Slash the fish 2 or 3 times on each side with a sharp knife and then rub in the marinade. Set aside for 30 minutes.

To make the spice crust, roast the coriander seeds, cumin seeds and black peppercorns in a dry frying pan for a few moments. Put them in a pestle and mortar or a food processor with all the remaining spice paste ingredients except the oil and mix them to a coarse paste, gradually adding the oil. Apply the spice crust to both sides of the fish to form an even coating. Use the leftover mixture to fill the belly of the fish.

Place the fish on a baking sheet and cook in an oven preheated to 200°C/400°F/Gas Mark 6 for 15–18 minutes, basting 2 or 3 times with the ghee or clarified butter. If the fish start to colour too much, reduce the temperature to 180°C/350°F/Gas Mark 4 and turn them over. You may need to cover them with foil towards the end to prevent the spice crust burning.

Serve with the lemon wedges, some Coriander Mash (see page 110) and/or a green salad.

CUMIN- AND CHILLI-CRUSTED SALMON STEAKS WITH GOAN XACUTI SAUCE

SERVES 6

4 x 200g (7-ounce) salmon steaks
I teaspoon sea salt
½ teaspoon black onion seeds
½ teaspoon cumin seeds, crushed
½ teaspoon coriander seeds, crushed
½ teaspoon dried red chilli flakes
2 tablespoons vegetable or corn oil
juice of ½ lemon

For the spice paste:
4 tablespoons vegetable or corn oil
80g (I cup) grated fresh coconut
6 garlic cloves, peeled
2.5cm (I-inch) piece of fresh ginger
2 tablespoons fresh coriander
2 tablespoons ground coriander
2 teaspoons poppy seeds, roasted in a
    dry frying pan
4 green chillies
I teaspoon red chilli powder
I teaspoon garam masala
½ teaspoon ground turmeric
I teaspoon crushed black peppercorns
½ teaspoon ground cumin

For the sauce:
2 tablespoons vegetable or corn oil
I onion, sliced
2 tablespoons malt vinegar
200ml (⁷⁄8 cup) fish stock or water
I tablespoon tamarind paste
2 teaspoons salt
2 tablespoons coconut milk

For its relatively small size, Goa has an extraordinary variety of culinary styles and influences. It is inhabited by Hindus, Muslims and Christians, who have all had an impact on its cooking. The food tends to be simple but chilli-hot. Xacuti is one of the milder dishes, and although it is made with chicken in some places, I find it works even better with salmon.

Pat the salmon steaks dry with kitchen paper. Mix the sea salt with the black onion seeds and half the cumin, coriander, chilli flakes and oil. Rub this mixture over the fish and set aside for 30 minutes.

For the spice paste, heat the oil in a heavy-based frying pan, add the coconut and roast until golden brown. Leave to cool, then add the rest of the ingredients and blend to a smooth paste in a food processor.

For the sauce, heat the oil in a deep frying pan, add the onion and sauté over a medium heat for 6–8 minutes, until golden brown. Add the spice paste and cook until the oil separates from the mixture. Add the vinegar, fish stock or water, tamarind and salt and simmer till the sauce becomes thick and smooth. Stir in the coconut milk and remove from the heat.

To cook the salmon, heat the remaining tablespoon of oil in a large, non-stick frying pan and place the fish in it, skin-side down. Cook for about 4–5 minutes on each side over a low to medium heat. Remove from the heat and press the remaining chilli flakes, crushed cumin and coriander on top of the fish. Place under a hot grill for a minute or two, until the spices release their flavour, then squeeze the lemon on top. Pour the sauce on to 4 warmed plates, add the salmon and serve. It goes well with rice or even a soft mash.

KEDGEREE WITH POACHED EGG AND SMOKED HADDOCK

SERVES 4

Kedgeree is a classic Anglo-Indian dish derived from the popular khichri – *rice and lentils cooked with ginger and onions. The British adapted it by adding eggs and smoked fish and it then made its way back to Britain as a breakfast dish, served in royal and aristocratic households with no greater a champion than Queen Victoria. Usually the eggs are just hard boiled and flaked into the rice but this version includes poached eggs as well, placed on top of the rice, which looks more dramatic.*

Put a quarter of the smoked haddock in a small pan, add enough milk to cover and bring slowly to the boil. Remove from the heat and set aside.

Heat the oil in a pan, add the onion and sauté till golden brown. Add the ginger and turmeric and cook for a minute, then add the stock or water. Toss in the boiled rice and heat through, then add the salt. Fold in the chopped egg whites. Flake the cooked haddock, removing any skin and bones, and add it to the pan with the coriander. Fold in the butter. Remove from the heat and keep warm.

Cut the remaining smoked haddock into 4 portions and place under a hot grill for 2–3 minutes on each side.

For the poached eggs, pour the water into a shallow pan, add the vinegar and salt and bring to a simmer. Carefully break in the eggs and simmer slowly until the whites coagulate and a thin film is formed over the yolk. You must take care that the water doesn't come to boiling point or the eggs will be ruined.

To serve, divide the rice between 4 serving bowls, put the haddock on top and the poached eggs on top of that.

200g (7 ounces) smoked haddock fillet
a little milk
1 tablespoon vegetable or corn oil
1 onion, chopped
1cm (½-inch) piece of fresh ginger, finely chopped
1 teaspoon ground turmeric
2 tablespoons hot fish stock or water
175g (scant 1 cup) basmati rice, boiled (see page 13)
1 teaspoon salt
whites from 2 hard-boiled eggs, chopped
1 tablespoon chopped fresh coriander
30g (2 tablespoons) butter

For the poached eggs:
1 litre (4 cups) water
2 tablespoons white vinegar
1 teaspoon salt
4 eggs

SEMOLINA-CRUSTED SEA BASS WITH CASHEW NUT SAUCE

SERVES 4

This recipe combines elements from two distinctly different parts of India. The semolina crust is a traditional cooking technique from the fishing community in Mumbai and all along the Western Ghats. Here it is combined with a nutty North Indian sauce made from cashew nut paste and yoghurt. You could substitute tilapia for the bass.

Pat the fish fillets dry on kitchen paper. Mix together all the ingredients for the marinade and rub them over the fish. Set aside for 30 minutes.

Meanwhile, make the sauce. Heat the oil in a heavy-based pan, add the onion and sauté till golden brown. Stir in the turmeric, followed by the cashew paste. Cook over a low heat, stirring constantly, until the oil separates from the mixture. Add the yoghurt a little at a time, stirring constantly, then cook over a moderate heat for 2 minutes. Add the fish stock, bring to the boil and simmer for another 6–8 minutes. Now add the ginger, salt and sugar and simmer until the oil starts to separate from the sauce around the edge of the pan. Stir in the lemon juice and fresh coriander, then set aside and keep warm.

Dust the fish fillets with the semolina. Heat the oil in a large frying pan and cook the fish (you will probably have to do it in batches) over a low heat for about 4–6 minutes on each side. If the fish starts to acquire too much colour before it is cooked through, transfer it to an oven preheated to 200°C/400°F/Gas Mark 6 and cook for 6–8 minutes.

Divide the sauce between 4 serving plates and put the fish on top. Serve with plain rice.

8 sea bass fillets
5 tablespoons coarse semolina
3 tablespoons vegetable or corn oil

For the marinade:
I tablespoon Ginger Paste (see page 12)
I tablespoon Garlic Paste (see page 12)
2 teaspoons red chilli powder
2 teaspoons salt
I tablespoon jaggery or molasses sugar
juice of I lemon

For the cashew nut sauce:
3 tablespoons vegetable or corn oil
I onion, finely chopped
I teaspoon ground turmeric
200g (I cup) Boiled Cashew Paste (see page 12)
120g (½ cup) plain yoghurt
600ml (2½ cups) fish stock
2.5cm (I-inch) piece of fresh ginger, finely chopped
I teaspoon salt
½ teaspoon sugar
juice of ½ lemon
I tablespoon chopped fresh coriander

PERCH IN RAJASTHANI YOGHURT SOUP

SERVES 6

This is the Cinnamon Club's version of a rare fish dish from Rajasthan. Traditionally Rajasthani cooking is biased towards lamb, goat, some poultry and fowl, historically a bit of game, but very little fish. Fish dishes were there more for the sake of variety than availability and it revolved around rohu, katla *or other freshwater varieties that might be available locally.*

Our rendition with perch is the closest you would get to what is otherwise called machhi ki kadhi *in Rajasthan. Nile perch is available frozen in Indian shops in the UK.*

Pat the fish pieces dry on kitchen paper. Mix together all the ingredients for the marinade, rub them over the fish and set aside for 20 minutes. Now sprinkle the gram flour and lemon juice over the fish and mix well with your hands.

To make the soup, whisk all the ingredients together, then pour into a saucepan, place over a medium heat and whisk. Lower the heat and cook for about 20 minutes, stirring occasionally, until the soup is glossy and smooth.

For the tempering, heat the oil in a small frying pan and add the cumin seeds, followed by the coriander seeds, asafoetida and red chillies. When they start to release their aroma, pour the tempering over the soup, sprinkle the fresh coriander on top and leave, covered with a lid, for a couple of minutes.

To cook the fish, heat the oil in a large frying pan, add the fish pieces and cook for about 2 minutes on each side, until golden brown (alternatively, you could deep-fry the fish for 2–3 minutes).

Divide the fish between 4 soup plates or bowls, pour the soup over and serve.

800g (1^{3}4 pounds) Nile perch fillets, cut into 16 pieces
2 tablespoons gram flour
juice of 1 lemon
4 tablespoons vegetable or corn oil

For the marinade;
1 teaspoon ground turmeric
1 teaspoon red chilli powder
½ teaspoon carom (ajowan) seeds
1½ teaspoons salt

For the soup:
60g (scant ½ cup) gram flour
½ teaspoon ground turmeric
1 teaspoon salt
600g (2½ cups) plain yoghurt
600ml (2½ cups) water

For the tempering:
1 tablespoon vegetable or corn oil
1 teaspoon cumin seeds
½ teaspoon coriander seeds
a pinch of asafoetida
6 dried red chillies
1 tablespoon chopped fresh coriander

BLACK COD AND CRAB KOFTA WITH KERALA CURRY SAUCE

SERVES 4

Black cod has a lovely delicate texture and melt-in-the-mouth butteriness that makes it more luxurious than ordinary cod. If you can't find any, though, by all means substitute any whte fish such as regular cod, haddock or pollack.

Heat half the oil in a frying pan and add the cumin seeds. When they begin to crackle, add the onion and sauté until soft. Add the ginger and green chillies and sauté for a minute. Stir in the crabmeat and salt and cook over a high heat until all the liquid evaporates. Remove from the heat and leave to cool. Mix in the minced cod, ground fennel and fresh coriander. Divide the mixture into 12 balls and flatten each one with the palm of your hand to make cakes about 1cm (1/2 inch) thick. Smooth the sides to get rid of any cracks that may appear, then cover and set aside.

To make the sauce, heat the oil in a pan, add the curry leaves and onion and sauté for 6–8 minutes, until the onion is golden brown. Add the chilli powder, tomatoes and salt and cook till the tomatoes disintegrate. Add the kokum berries and fish stock or water and simmer for 2–3 minutes. Stir in the coconut milk and simmer for 2–3 minutes longer, until the sauce has a creamy consistency. Taste and add the sugar if necessary.

To finish the koftas, heat the remaining 2 tablespoons of oil in a large frying pan, place the koftas in it and cook over a low heat for about 2–3 minutes on each side, until golden brown. Serve with the sauce, some plain rice and, if you like, Spinach and Coconut Porial (see page 113).

4 tablespoons vegetable or corn oil
I teaspoon cumin seeds
I large onion, chopped
2.5cm (I-inch) piece of fresh ginger, finely chopped
4 green chillies, chopped
300g (II ounces) fresh crabmeat, preferably hand picked
2 teaspoons salt
500g (I pound 2 ounces) skinned black cod fillet, minced
I teaspoon fennel seeds, roasted in a dry frying pan and ground
2 tablespoons chopped fresh coriander

For the Kerala curry sauce:
3 tablespoons vegetable or corn oil
IO fresh curry leaves
I large onion, finely chopped
I tablespoon mild red chilli powder
2 tomatoes, finely chopped
I teaspoon salt
2 kokum berries (or 2 tablespoons tamarind paste)
3 tablespoons fish stock or water
200ml ($^7/8$ cup) coconut milk
$^1/2$ teaspoon sugar (optional)

SEARED SCALLOPS WITH TAMARIND AND CHILLI, MUNG BEAN KEDGEREE

SERVES 4

This is a wonderful dish that involves various cooking techniques, all of which add different colours, flavours and textures. It's a great way to impress your guests over a dinner table!

First make the kedgeree. Wash the yellow mung beans, put them in a pan with the water and turmeric and bring to the boil. Simmer until the beans dissolve completely and the liquid has reduced by about half. Remove from the heat and blend to a purée with a hand-held blender, then set aside.

Heat the ghee or butter in a pan and add the cumin seeds. Add the onion and sauté until it begins to colour, then add the ginger and green chillies and cook for a minute. Stir in the cooked mung beans, salt and cream, then fold in the cooked rice and the sprouted mung beans, if using. Add the tomato and coriander and stir over a low heat for 3–4 minutes. Remove from the heat, spread the butter on top and keep warm.

To cook the scallops, heat the oil in a large, heavy-based frying pan over a high heat, add the scallops and sear for about 1½ minutes on each side, until golden brown. Sprinkle the salt on top and remove from the pan. Mix together the tamarind paste, coriander and cumin seeds and chilli flakes and spread them evenly on top of the scallops. Place under a hot grill for a minute or two, until the tamarind paste begins to caramelise.

Stir the butter into the kedgeree and divide between 4 plates. Place the scallops on top and serve, accompanied by Tapioca Chips (see page 113).

2 tablespoons vegetable or corn oil
20 fresh king scallops
1 teaspoon salt
2 tablespoons tamarind paste
1 tablespoon coriander seeds, roasted in a dry frying pan and crushed
1 tablespoon cumin seeds, roasted in a dry frying pan and crushed
1½ teaspoons red chilli flakes

For the mung bean kedgeree:
100g (½ cup) yellow mung beans
500ml (2 cups) water
a pinch of ground turmeric
2 tablespoons ghee or clarified butter
½ teaspoon cumin seeds
1 large onion, finely chopped
1cm (½-inch) piece of fresh ginger, finely chopped
2 green chillies, finely chopped
1 teaspoon salt
4 tablespoons single cream
60g (heaping ⅓ cup) basmati rice, boiled (see page 13) and cooled
50g (¼ cup) sprouted green mung beans (optional)
1 tomato, deseeded and cut into 1cm (½-inch) dice
2 tablespoons chopped fresh coriander
15g (1 tablespoon) salted butter

KERALA-STYLE BIRYANI WITH MUSSELS AND MONKFISH

SERVES 4

This is an adaptation of the traditional mopla biryani prepared by the Muslim population in Kerala. They would use a meaty fish like swordfish or tuna but I like to use monkfish. Its firm texture goes beautifully with the spices.

Pat the monkfish pieces dry on kitchen paper. Mix together all the marinade ingredients, rub them over the fish and set aside for 30 minutes.

Heat the oil in a large frying pan, add the monkfish pieces and fry for a minute or two, until golden brown (cook them in batches if necessary, so as not to overcrowd the pan).

Remove the monkfish from the pan, add the sliced onions to the oil and sauté until golden brown. Add the ginger, garlic and green chilli pastes and sauté for a minute, then stir in the chopped tomato and cook until soft. Add the yoghurt, coconut milk, coriander and salt and simmer for about 5 minutes. Now return the monkfish to the pan, add the garam masala and mussels, mix well and remove from the heat.

Wash the rice, then leave it to soak in a large bowl of cold water for 20 minutes. Meanwhile, heat half the ghee or butter in a large pan, add the cardamom, cinnamon, cloves, peppercorns and bay leaves and stir until they release their fragrance. Add the onion and sauté until golden brown. Add the water and salt and bring to the boil. Drain the rice and add to the pan, reduce the heat and cook for 6–8 minutes, until the rice is about three-quarters done.

Put half the seafood mixture in a heavy-based casserole. Drain the rice and spread half of it over the seafood. Repeat with the rest of the seafood and rice. Sprinkle the remaining ghee or butter on top of the rice and cover the casserole with a tight-fitting lid. Seal the sides with foil, leaving a small gap for steam to escape. Cook over a high heat for 5 minutes, until you see the steam through the gap. Reduce to a very low heat and cook for another 10 minutes. Remove from the heat and leave to stand for 5 minutes. Carefully remove the lid and serve the biryani with Spiced Onion Yoghurt (see page 114).

500g (1 pound 2 ounces) monkfish, cut into 12 pieces
5 tablespoons vegetable or corn oil
3 red onions, sliced
1 tablespoon Ginger Paste (see page 12)
1 tablespoon Garlic Paste (see page 12)
10–12 green chillies, stalks removed and made into a paste in a mortar and pestle
1 tomato, chopped
1 tablespoon Greek yoghurt
120ml (½ cup) coconut milk
3 tablespoons chopped fresh coriander
1 tablespoon salt
1 tablespoon garam masala
500g (1 pound 2 ounces) mussels, scrubbed and de-bearded

For the marinade:
1 teaspoon red chilli powder
½ teaspoon ground turmeric
1 teaspoon salt

For the rice:
250g (1¼ cups) basmati rice
4 tablespoons ghee or clarified butter
4 green cardamom pods
4 cinnamon sticks
4 cloves
10 black peppercorns
2 bay leaves
1 red onion, sliced
2.5 litres (2½ quarts) water
1 tablespoon salt

WILD PRAWNS SIMMERED IN CHILLI, TOMATO AND LIME SAUCE

SERVES 6

Wild prawns are a delight if you can get hold of some. At the Cinnamon Club, we often get wild prawns caught off the African coast and they are just huge. They are ideal for grilling or even added to curries, as they retain their texture very well.

Heat the ghee or butter in a pan, add the bay leaf and sieved tomatoes and simmer for 5 minutes. In a bowl, mix the ginger and garlic pastes, red chilli powder and cumin with a little water to make a smooth paste. Add this mixture to the pan and simmer for 5 minutes, stirring to prevent sticking. Stir in the coconut milk, lemongrass, fennel and coriander seeds. Add the salt, sugar and lime leaves and simmer for 3–4 minutes. Add the prawns and simmer for another 6–8 minutes, until the prawns are cooked and the sauce is infused with the lemongrass and lime leaf flavour. Serve with plain rice.

75g (⅓ cup) ghee or clarified butter
1 bay leaf
6 ripe tomatoes, boiled in a little water until tender, then blended and passed through a sieve to make a purée
1 teaspoon Ginger Paste (see page 12)
1 teaspoon Garlic Paste (see page 12)
1 teaspoon red chilli powder
1 teaspoon ground cumin
300ml (1¼ cups) coconut milk
1 lemongrass stick
1 teaspoon fennel seeds
1 teaspoon coriander seeds, roasted in a dry frying pan
1½ teaspoons salt
1 teaspoon sugar
4 fresh kaffir lime leaves
800g (1¾ pounds) raw headless wild or seawater prawns, peeled and de-veined, with the tail shell left intact

SEAFOOD 'KHICHRI'

SERVES 4

This dish is the mother of the Anglo-Indian version of kedgeree (see page 77). The humble khichri, *as it is known all over the Subcontinent, is essentially a light, one-dish meal, easy to digest and particularly useful for convalescents. Traditionally it would have been cooked for so long that the rice and lentils would become completely mashed together, but I like to cook it slightly less, so that you can still distinguish between the different textures.*

Wash the mung beans, put them in a saucepan with the fish stock or water and the turmeric and bring to the boil. Simmer until the beans have completely disintegrated. Mix well with the remaining cooking liquid to give a rough purée, then remove from the heat and set aside.

Heat 60g (4 tablespoons) of the ghee or butter in a heavy-based pan and add the cumin seeds. When they crackle, add the onions and sauté until they begin to turn golden brown. Stir in the ginger, green chillies and salt and sauté for a minute. Add the prawns and cook for 2–3 minutes. Now add the pieces of white fish and cook for another 3 minutes. Stir in the boiled mung beans and bring to the boil. Add the squid, mussels and tomatoes and cook for another 2–3 minutes, until the mussels have opened.

Fold in the cooked rice, taking care not to break up the fish. When the rice is heated through, finish with the remaining ghee or butter and sprinkle in the coriander and lemon juice. Remove from the heat and serve immediately.

200g (1 cup) split yellow mung beans
1 litre (4 cups) fish stock or water
a pinch of ground turmeric
75g (⅓ cup) ghee or clarified butter
1 teaspoon cumin seeds
2 onions, chopped
2.5cm (1-inch) piece of fresh ginger, finely chopped
4 green chillies, finely chopped
1 tablespoon salt
100g (4 ounces) shelled raw prawns
200g (7 ounces) white fish fillet, such as halibut, cod or pollock, skinned and cut into 2.5cm (1-inch) dice
100g (4 ounces) cleaned squid, cut into rings
200g (7 ounces) fresh mussels, scrubbed and de-bearded
2 tomatoes, deseeded and cut into 1cm (½-inch) dice
75g (scant ½ cup) basmati rice, boiled (see page 13)
2 tablespoons chopped fresh coriander
juice of 1 lemon

TANDOORI-STYLE KING PRAWNS WITH FENNEL AND CORIANDER SEEDS

SERVES 6

Cooking in a tandoor oven isn't exactly practical at home, so when I was adapting recipes for The Cinnamon Club Cookbook *(Absolute Press, 2003) I devised a double-marinade technique, which gives very similar results to a tandoor. The prawns are marinated briefly, then fried before being coated in a second marinade and baked.*

For this recipe I suggest you try to find freshwater king prawns – the larger the better. You could use seawater prawns but freshwater ones hold the marinade better and taste sweeter and juicier.

If you had smaller prawns and took off the tail shells, you could serve them as a party snack on the skewers.

Soak 4 bamboo skewers in water for about 30 minutes. Put the prawns in a bowl, mix in all the ingredients for the first marinade and set aside for 10 minutes.

Heat the oil in a large, heavy-based frying pan, add the prawns and sear quickly over a high heat so that they curl up. Remove from the heat immediately and set aside to cool.

Mix all the ingredients for the second marinade together and dip the prawns in it. Thread the prawns on the bamboo skewers, piercing the skewer through the tail of each prawn and taking it out through the top. Place on a baking sheet and bake for 5–6 minutes in an oven preheated to 200°C/400°F/Gas Mark 6. Then place under a hot grill for 1 minute, until browned. Serve with a salad of your choice.

500g (I pound 2 ounces) raw headless king prawns, peeled and de-veined, with the tail shell left intact
I tablespoon vegetable or corn oil

For the first marinade:
I teaspoon Ginger Paste (see page 12)
I teaspoon Garlic Paste (see page 12)
½ teaspoon ground turmeric
I teaspoon salt
½ teaspoon finely ground white pepper

For the second marinade:
2 tablespoons Greek yoghurt
I tablespoon cream cheese
I tablespoon single cream
Icm (½-inch) piece of fresh ginger, finely chopped
I green chilli, finely chopped
I tablespoon chopped fresh coriander
I teaspoon Mace and Cardamom Powder (see page 12)
I teaspoon salt
I tablespoon fennel seeds, roasted in a dry frying pan and then crushed
I tablespoon coriander seeds, roasted in a dry frying pan and then crushed

KING CRAB CLAWS WITH GARLIC AND PEPPER BUTTER

SERVES 4

The monsters in question here, king crabs, are found in Barents Sea, north of Norway and just south of the Arctic Circle. These crabs are huge, and just the clusters of their claws can be up to half a metre in length. They are scavengers and feed on whatever is available on the seabed.

In recent times their population has grown and is affecting the marine life of its surroundings – so much so that the Norwegian Seafood Board is trying to create more of an awareness of the king crab to increase its consumption in the international market. It should not be too difficult, as the meat is delicious and sweet and, what's more, there's lots of it! Each of the digits from the claw clusters has more meat than the average lobster.

King crab claws are not universally available but I believe they soon will be. In the meantime, if you are having difficulties in supply, you could always try this recipe with whole crabs or lobster, removing the meat from the shells and cutting it into chunks.

800g (1¾ pounds) king crab claws, separated at the digits and cut in half lengthways (you could ask your fishmonger to do this)
1 tablespoon melted salted butter
1 teaspoon salt
1 teaspoon ground green cardamom
½ teaspoon sugar
1 tablespoon coconut milk
1 tablespoon chopped fresh coriander
juice of 1 lemon

For the garlic and pepper butter:
2 tablespoons vegetable or corn oil
2 garlic cloves, finely chopped
1 onion, finely chopped
2 green chillies, finely chopped
½ teaspoon black peppercorns, crushed
3 tablespoons fish stock or water
1 teaspoon salt
½ teaspoon sugar
25g (2 tablespoons) butter, diced
juice of 1 lemon
1 tablespoon chopped chives

Arrange the prepared crab claws on a baking tray, flesh-side up, and brush them with the melted butter. Sprinkle with the salt, cardamom and sugar and drizzle with the coconut milk, then set aside.

For the garlic and pepper butter, heat the oil in a heavy-based pan, add the garlic and sauté until softened but not coloured. Add the onion and green chillies and cook, covered, over a low heat. When the onion is soft, add the peppercorns and stock or water and simmer for 2–3 minutes. Mix in the salt and sugar, then whisk in the butter a little at a time to form a thick emulsion. Take care not to let the sauce boil or the butter will split. Squeeze in the lemon juice, sprinkle in the chives and keep warm.

Place the seasoned claws under a hot grill for 8–10 minutes, until golden. Remove from the grill and sprinkle with the coriander and lemon juice. Serve immediately, with the garlic and pepper butter.

INDIAN CLASSICS

HAKE IN BENGALI DOPIAZA SAUCE

CATFISH IN MUSTARD, COCONUT AND CHILLI SAUCE

MACKEREL IN MANGALORE-STYLE
CORIANDER AND PEPPER SAUCE

HYDERABADI-STYLE FISH KORMA

ANDHRA-STYLE SEAFOOD CURRY

SILVER POMFRET FILLED WITH SHRIMP

ALLEPPEY-STYLE SEAFOOD CURRY WITH GREEN
MANGO AND COCONUT

FRESHWATER KING PRAWNS IN MALAI CURRY SAUCE

HAKE IN BENGALI DOPIAZA SAUCE

SERVES 4

The term dopiaza *is frequently used in Indian cooking and means different things in different parts of the country. It could refer to the quantity of onions used in relation to the rest of the ingredients or to the addition of onions at two different stages of the cooking, which gives two distinctly different textures. In this recipe, it refers to the latter.*

Pat the fish pieces dry on kitchen paper, rub in the salt, onion seeds and half the oil and set aside for 30 minutes.

To make the sauce, heat the oil in a large frying pan and add the mustard seeds. When they begin to crackle, add the onion and sauté till soft. Add the turmeric and cumin and sauté for a minute. Add the yoghurt a little at a time, stirring constantly to prevent it splitting. Pour in the fish stock or water and bring to a simmer. Cook over a low to medium heat until the liquid has reduced by half, then add the mustard, salt and sugar and cook for 2 minutes.

Add the tomato, green chillies and fresh coriander and cook for another 2 minutes. Stir in the Greek yoghurt, then remove from the heat and keep warm.

For the garnish, heat the clarified butter and the oil in a pan and toss the sliced red onion in it. Stir-fry quickly over a high heat to caramelise the outside of the onion but still retain its crunch. Drain on kitchen paper and keep warm.

To cook the fish, heat the rest of the oil in a large frying pan, place the hake pieces in it, skin-side down, and cook over a medium heat for 3–5 minutes. Transfer the fish to a baking tray, brush the top with the clarified butter and place under a hot grill for 3–4 minutes, until the fish is well cooked. Garnish with the crunchy red onions and serve with the sauce and some plain rice.

4 x 200g (7-ounce) pieces of hake fillet
I teaspoon salt
½ teaspoon black onion seeds
2 tablespoons vegetable or corn oil
I½ teaspoons clarified butter

For the sauce:
2 tablespoons mustard or corn oil
2 teaspoons mustard seeds
I red onion, sliced Icm (½ inch) thick
½ teaspoon ground turmeric
I teaspoon cumin seeds, roasted in a
    dry frying pan and then ground
2 tablespoons plain yoghurt
400ml (I²/₃ cups) fish stock or water
I tablespoon kasundi mustard or I½
    tablespoons wholegrain English
    mustard
2 teaspoons salt
I teaspoon sugar
I tomato, cut into 8 and deseeded
4 green chillies, slit lengthways in half
I tablespoon chopped fresh coriander
4 tablespoons Greek yoghurt

For the garnish:
I½ teaspoons clarified butter
I tablespoon vegetable or corn oil
I red onion, sliced Icm (½ inch) thick

CATFISH IN MUSTARD, COCONUT AND CHILLI SAUCE

SERVES 4

This authentic Bengali dish is unusual for its simplicity – there is none of the usual grinding of complex pastes and lengthy cooking. Although catfish is traditional, almost any other fish would work just as well. You could try rohu *or* katla *(both available frozen from Bengali shops), or you could even use halibut.*

Pat the catfish steaks dry on kitchen paper. Mix together all the ingredients for the marinade and rub them over the fish. Set aside for 20 minutes.

To make the spice mix, roast all the ingredients in a dry frying pan until they release their aroma, then pound them to a coarse powder in a mortar and pestle. Dust the fish with this spice mix and set aside for 10 minutes.

For the sauce, put the mustard oil or ghee, mustard, coconut milk, yoghurt, stock or water, salt, turmeric and chillies in a small pan and stir constantly over a low heat until the mixture comes to a boil. Simmer for 5–6 minutes, until it thickens, then check the seasoning. Add the sugar, if required, to balance the sourness.

To cook the catfish, heat the oil in a large, ovenproof frying pan and add the fish steaks. Cook over a low to medium heat for about 5 minutes on each side. Add the butter and lemon juice, then transfer the pan to an oven preheated to 180°C/350°F/Gas Mark 4 and cook for 4–5 minutes (alternatively you could sear the fish as above and then simmer it in the sauce until cooked). Sprinkle the garam masala and ginger over the fish, then serve with the sauce and some plain rice.

4 x 180g (6-ounce) catfish steaks (on or off the bone)
2 tablespoons vegetable or corn oil
15g (1 tablespoon) butter
juice of 1 lemon
a pinch of garam masala
1cm (½-inch) piece of fresh ginger, cut into fine shreds

For the marinade:
1 tablespoon Ginger Paste (see page 12)
1 tablespoon Garlic Paste (see page 12)
2 teaspoons red chilli powder
1 teaspoon ground turmeric
1½ teaspoons salt

For the spice mix:
1 tablespoon coriander seeds
1 teaspoon cumin seeds
1 teaspoon black peppercorns
½ teaspoon fenugreek seeds

For the sauce:
1 tablespoon mustard oil or ghee
3 tablespoons kasundi mustard (or wholegrain Dijon mustard)
150ml (²/3 cup) coconut milk
2 tablespoons plain yoghurt
200ml (⁷/8 cup) fish stock or water
½ teaspoon salt
½ teaspoon ground turmeric
4 green chillies, slit open lengthways
a pinch of sugar (optional)

MACKEREL IN MANGALORE-STYLE CORIANDER AND PEPPER SAUCE

SERVES 4

This coastal recipe from the Western Ghats is very rich and spicy. The spice paste serves the dual purpose of flavouring the dish and thickening the sauce.

Wash the mackerel fillets, pat them dry on kitchen paper, then cut them in half. Mix together the salt, turmeric and chilli powder, rub them over the mackerel and set aside for 20 minutes. Heat the oil in a large frying pan, add the mackerel fillets skin-side down and fry for 2 minutes on each side (do this in batches if necessary). Remove from the heat and set aside.

Put all the ingredients for the spice paste in a food processor, add a little water and blend to a smooth paste. Set aside.

For the sauce, heat the oil and butter in a large, heavy-based pan, add the whole spices and let them crackle until the aroma is released. Add the chopped onion and stir until golden brown. Add the garlic and ginger, followed by the spice paste, and stir till the fat begins to separate from the mixture and the sauce turns golden brown. Add the fish stock or water, tamarind paste and salt and bring to a simmer.

Cook over a low heat until the sauce thickens. Add the mackerel fillets to the sauce, bring it back to a simmer and finish with the lemon juice, coconut milk and the sugar if you think it needs it. Serve with plain rice or Lemon Rice (see page 106).

8 mackerel fillets, pin boned
I teaspoon salt
I teaspoon ground turmeric
I teaspoon red chilli powder
3 tablespoons vegetable or corn oil

For the spice paste:
80g (I cup) grated fresh coconut
I teaspoon ground coriander
½ teaspoon red chilli powder
½ teaspoon ground turmeric
½ teaspoon garam masala
I teaspoon ground fennel seeds
½ teaspoon fenugreek seeds, roasted in a dry frying pan and then ground
I teaspoon crushed black peppercorns
5 garlic cloves, peeled
5cm (2-inch) piece of fresh ginger, roughly chopped

For the coriander and pepper sauce:
I tablespoon groundnut or corn oil
25g (2 tablespoons) butter
5cm (2-inch) piece of cinnamon stick
3 green cardamom pods
5 cloves
3 star anise
I red onion, finely chopped
2 garlic cloves, chopped
2.5cm (I-inch) piece of fresh ginger, chopped
200ml (⅞ cup) fish stock (or water)
2 tablespoons tamarind paste
2 teaspoons salt
juice of ½ lemon
2 tablespoons coconut milk
I teaspoon sugar (optional)

HYDERABADI-STYLE FISH KORMA

SERVES 4

This is a very special classic Indian dish, one of the few fish dishes to feature in the royal cooking of the Nizams, the Muslim rulers of Hyderabad. It's rather delicate and elaborate but well worth the effort.

To make the spice paste, soak all the ingredients in enough warm water to cover for about 30 minutes, then blend to a fine paste in a blender or food processor.

Pat the fish pieces dry on kitchen paper, rub in 1 teaspoon of the salt and the turmeric and set aside for 20 minutes. Heat half the ghee or clarified butter in a large, heavy-based frying pan, add the fish fillets and fry gently for 2–3 minutes on each side, until they are golden brown. Remove from the pan and drain on kitchen paper.

Heat the remaining ghee or clarified butter in the same pan, add the ground spice paste and fry over a medium heat till it is brown and releases its aroma. Slowly add the yoghurt, stirring constantly over a low heat. Keep stirring until the ghee leaves the sides of the pan. Add the hot water and bring to the boil, then reduce the heat and simmer for 5 minutes. Add the fish and the remaining salt, stir gently, then cover and cook over a low heat for about 5 minutes. Gently stir in the saffron milk and sugar, then sprinkle in the fresh coriander, mint and lemon juice. Cover and cook over a very low heat for about 2 minutes. Stir in the double cream, remove from the heat and serve with plain rice.

4 x 200g (7-ounce) white fish fillets, such as halibut, cod or pollock
2 teaspoons salt
½ teaspoon ground turmeric
4 tablespoons ghee or clarified butter
200g (⅞ cup) yoghurt, whisked to remove any lumps
300ml (1¼ cups) hot water
½ teaspoon saffron strands, infused in 2 tablespoons warm milk
1 teaspoon sugar
1 tablespoon chopped fresh coriander
1 tablespoon chopped mint
juice of ½ lemon
4 tablespoons double cream

For the spice paste:
4 dried red chillies, deseeded
2 large onions, finely chopped
2.5cm (1-inch) piece of fresh ginger, sliced
4 garlic cloves, peeled
2 green chillies, chopped
1 teaspoon black peppercorns
5 cloves
3 green cardamom pods
5cm (2-inch) piece of cinnamon stick
2 teaspoons coriander seeds
1 teaspoon cumin seeds
2 teaspoons poppy seeds
½ teaspoon ground turmeric
2 teaspoons garam masala
2 tablespoons blanched almonds

ANDHRA-STYLE SEAFOOD CURRY

SERVES 4

This is quite a special dish in that it requires an understanding of the various textures of the different seafood used. It's also special in the way it's finished with a tempering of garlic and fenugreek. This is quite unusual for fish dishes in India.

First prepare the masala. Dry roast all the ingredients in a moderately hot frying pan for a minute or two, until they are just dried but not coloured. Remove from the heat and grind to a powder in a mortar and pestle or an electric grinder, then set aside.

Heat 2 tablespoons of the oil in a large pan and add the mustard seeds. When they crackle, add the curry leaves, immediately followed by the chopped onions, and sauté till golden. Now add the turmeric, chilli powder and tamarind paste and sauté for 2 minutes. Add the tomatoes and cook for 5 minutes.

Add the diced white fish and the prawns and sauté for 1 minute. Pour in the water or fish stock and simmer for 2–3 minutes. Now add the Andhra masala and simmer for another 2 minutes. Add the squid, then the mussels. Stir in the salt and check the seasoning. Reduce the heat to a slow simmer and cook for 2 minutes. Take care not to cook the dish too long after adding the squid and mussels or they will be overcooked.

In a separate pan, heat the remaining tablespoon of oil, add the garlic and fenugreek seeds and fry over a high heat for just under a minute. Transfer to a mortar and pestle and pound to a coarse paste. Add this mixture to the seafood curry, along with the slit green chillies, lemon juice and fresh coriander. Cover and leave to rest for 5 minutes, then serve with plain rice.

3 tablespoons groundnut or vegetable oil
I teaspoon mustard seeds
I sprig of fresh curry leaves
3 red onions, chopped
I teaspoon ground turmeric
I teaspoon red chilli powder
I tablespoon tamarind paste
4 tomatoes, chopped
200g (7 ounces) halibut, monkfish or similar meaty fish, cut into 2.5cm (I-inch) dice
450g (I pound) large freshwater prawns, peeled and de-veined
300ml (I¼ cups) water or fish stock
200g (7 ounces) cleaned squid, cut into rings Icm (½ inch) thick
20 mussels, scrubbed and de-bearded
I½ teaspoons salt
6 garlic cloves, sliced
I teaspoon fenugreek seeds
6 green chillies, slit open lengthways
juice of I lemon
I tablespoon chopped fresh coriander

For the Andhra masala:
2 tablespoons desiccated coconut
4 dried red chillies
I teaspoon cumin seeds
I teaspoon coriander seeds
I teaspoon white poppy seeds
5cm (2-inch) piece of cinnamon stick
2 bay leaves
2 green cardamom pods

SILVER POMFRET FILLED WITH SHRIMP

SERVES 4

Pomfret is probably the most popular fish in India – no menu would be complete without it. So much so that even restaurants like the famous Dumpukht in the Sheraton Hotel in New Delhi, which showcases the traditional cuisine of Lucknow, serve pomfret, despite the fact that it is not to be found anywhere near Lucknow!

You could try this dish with small John Dory. It calls for considerable skill in boning the fish, so make sure you have plenty of time – or ask your fishmonger to do it.

Pat dry each pomfret and insert the tip of a very sharp knife through the incision in the belly. Work the knife along the centre bone to release the flesh from the bone. Run your knife all along the centre bone and work all the way to the back of the fish, taking care not to tear the fish through. Turn the fish over and repeat the process on the other side. When the flesh has been released from the bone on both sides, use kitchen scissors to snip through the bone at the head and tail end. Carefully remove the bone to obtain a whole fish complete with head and tail but without any bone in the centre. The pocket created by removing the bone will be filled with the shrimp mixture.

Mix together all the ingredients for the marinade and rub them all over the fish. Set aside for 15 minutes.

Meanwhile, make the filling. Heat the oil in a frying pan and add the cumin seeds. When they crackle, add the red onion and sauté for 3–5 minutes, until light golden. Then add the ginger, chillies, turmeric and salt. Add the shrimps and cook for another minute or so, then add the coriander and garam masala. Remove from the heat and leave to cool. Stir in the grated cheese.

Stuff the pomfret with the shrimp mixture. Brush the edges of the cavity with the beaten egg and press gently together, pushing the filling as far back in the cavity as possible without tearing the fish and being careful to maintain its shape. Chill for 15 minutes.

For the batter, put all the dry ingredients into a bowl, then gradually whisk in the vinegar and water. In a deep-fat fryer or a large, deep saucepan, heat some oil to 180°C/350°F. Dip the fish in the batter and deep-fry, one at a time, for 6–8 minutes, taking care that the cavity does not open up. Make sure the fish does not colour too quickly or it will be too dark after it has been cooked in the oven.

Drain on kitchen paper. When you have fried all the fish, arrange them on a baking sheet and finish cooking in an oven preheated to 180°C/350°F/Gas Mark 4 for 5–6 minutes. Remove from the oven, sprinkle with the chaat masala and serve with the lemon wedges.

4 x 300g (11-ounce) whole pomfret, cleaned
1 egg, lightly beaten
oil for deep-frying
1 teaspoon chaat masala
1 lemon, cut into wedges, to serve

For the marinade:
1½ teaspoons Ginger Paste (see page 12)
1½ teaspoons Garlic Paste (see page 12)
juice of 1 lemon
1 teaspoon ground turmeric
1 teaspoon red chilli powder
1 teaspoon salt

For the filling:
2 tablespoons vegetable or corn oil
1 teaspoon black cumin or royal cumin seeds
1 red onion, finely chopped
2.5cm (1-inch) piece of fresh ginger, finely chopped
4 green chillies, finely chopped
½ teaspoon ground turmeric
1 teaspoon salt
200g (7 ounces) shelled cooked shrimps
1 tablespoon chopped fresh coriander
½ teaspoon garam masala
50g (½cup) Cheddar cheese, grated

For the batter:
5 tablespoons cornflour
100g rice flour
1 tablespoon red chilli powder
1 teaspoon salt
1 teaspoon crushed black peppercorns
2 garlic cloves, finely chopped
½ tablespoon finely chopped chives
50ml (3½ tablespoons) white vinegar
180ml (¾ cup) sparkling water

ALLEPPEY-STYLE SEAFOOD CURRY WITH GREEN MANGO AND COCONUT

SERVES 4-6

Alleppey is a small town some miles from Cochin. Of the dozens of ways in which fish curry is cooked in Kerala, this is one of the most interesting. It uses green mango as a souring agent rather than tamarind or kokum. Together with the coconut, it lends a beautiful freshness and lightness, which is superior to all other versions.

To make the spice paste, put all the ingredients in a food processor or blender and blend to a smooth paste. Set aside.

For the sauce, heat the oil in a deep frying pan and add the mustard seeds. When they begin to crackle, add the garlic, ginger, green chillies and curry leaves. Stir quickly, without letting the garlic colour. Add the shallots, followed by the mangoes, and sauté till they are soft. Stir in the spice paste, salt and fish stock or water and bring to a simmer.

Now add the prawns and cook for 2–3 minutes. As the sauce thickens, add the salmon and white fish and cook for another 2–3 minutes. Add the squid and mix with the rest of the fish. Allow the liquid to come back to a simmer and then add the mussels. Simmer only until the mussels have opened up, then stir in the coconut milk and remove from the heat. Take care not to cook the curry for too long after adding the squid and mussels as they overcook easily. Serve with plain rice.

200g (7 ounces) headless raw prawns, peeled and de-veined
200g (7 ounces) salmon fillet, cut into 2.5cm (1-inch) dice
200g (7 ounces) white fish fillet, such as halibut, cod or pollock, cut into 2.5cm (1-inch) dice
100g (4 ounces) cleaned squid, cut into rings
200g (7 ounces) mussels, scrubbed and de-bearded
2 tablespoons coconut milk

For the spice paste:
80g (1 cup) grated fresh coconut
1 teaspoon ground turmeric
1½ teaspoons red chilli powder
120ml (½ cup) water

For the sauce:
3 tablespoons coconut oil or vegetable oil
½ teaspoon mustard seeds
5 garlic cloves, cut into fine strips
2.5cm (1-inch) piece of fresh ginger, cut into fine strips
4 green chillies, cut lengthways in half
10 fresh curry leaves
5 shallots, sliced
2 green mangoes, peeled, pitted and sliced
1½ teaspoons salt
600ml (2½ cups) fish stock or water

LOBSTER BIRYANI WITH DILL

SERVES 4

Traditionally biryanis were considered a rather 'rough' meal, and were generally made with tough cuts of meat or poultry. It is certainly not common to see many seafood versions other than in the coastal regions of India. This lobster biryani, however, is a rather exceptional dish, to be reserved for special occasions. The inclusion of dill with Indian spices adds an interesting dimension to it.

Twist off the claws from the lobsters, crack them open and remove the meat. Remove the meat from the body, then cut all the meat into 2.5cm (1-inch) pieces. Pat dry on kitchen paper.

For the marinade, fry the onion in the oil until golden, then drain, reserving the oil. Mix the onion with all the remaining marinade ingredients. Add the lobster, coat it well in the marinade and set aside for 30 minutes.

Pour the reserved oil over the lobster. Wash the basmati rice, then leave it to soak in a large bowl of cold water for 20 minutes.

Fill a large pan with the water, add the whole spices and salt and bring to the boil. Drain the rice, add it to the pan and boil for 6–8 minutes, until it is about three-quarters cooked.

Place the marinated lobster in a large, heavy-based casserole. Drain the rice and arrange it in a layer over the lobster, sprinkling the chopped dill and mint on top. Pour the ghee or clarified butter, the saffron-infused milk and the rosewater over the rice and then cover the pot with a tight-fitting lid. Seal the sides with aluminium foil, leaving a small gap for steam to escape. Set the sealed casserole over a high heat for 4–5 minutes, until you see the steam through the gap. Reduce the heat to low and cook for another 3–5 minutes. Remove from the heat and leave to stand for 5 minutes.

Remove the lid carefully and serve straight away. It is a good idea to open the pot at the table, so everyone can enjoy the moment when the aromas are released.

2 live lobsters, cut in half lengthways and cleaned (you can ask your fishmonger to do this, as long as you cook the lobsters on the same day)

For the marinade
1 large onion, sliced
3 tablespoons vegetable or corn oil
8 green chillies, stalks removed, made into a paste in a mortar and pestle
1½ teaspoons Ginger Paste (see page 12)
1½ teaspoons Garlic Paste (see page 12)
2.5cm (1-inch) piece of fresh ginger, cut into fine matchsticks
½ teaspoon ground turmeric
1 teaspoon garam masala
1 tablespoon salt
2 tablespoons plain yoghurt
2 tablespoons single cream
1 tablespoon chopped fresh coriander
2 tablespoons ghee or clarified butter

For the rice:
250g (1¼ cups) basmati rice
2.5 litres (2½ quarts) water
4 green cardamom pods
4 cinnamon sticks
4 cloves
10 black peppercorns
2 bay leaves
1 tablespoon salt
1 tablespoon chopped dill
1 tablespoon chopped mint
3 tablespoons ghee or clarified butter
a large pinch of saffron strands, soaked in 3 tablespoons warm milk
1 tablespoon rosewater

FRESHWATER KING PRAWNS IN MALAI CURRY SAUCE

SERVES 4

This is one of the most sought-after seafood dishes in Bengal, reserved for important guests and very special occasions, such as weddings. Some versions are presented in the shell of a tender green coconut. The term malai *refers to the creamy, tender meat inside a young coconut.*

Heat 2 tablespoons of the ghee in a large, heavy-based pan and add the bay leaves and cardamom pods. When the cardamom pods change colour, add the onion paste and cook over a low heat until it turns light brown, stirring constantly to prevent sticking. Add the ginger paste, garlic paste, turmeric and cumin and sauté for 3–4 minutes. Add the prawns and toss well to coat them in the mixture.

Pour in the coconut milk and bring to a simmer, then add the slit green chillies and the salt. Simmer for 8–10 minutes over a low heat, until the prawns are cooked. If the sauce becomes too thick, dilute it with a little water and simmer until the sauce becomes consistent and flavours are well blended. Add the fresh coconut meat if you are using it.

To finish, sprinkle the ground cardamom over the top, with the sugar, if using, and stir in the remaining spoonful of ghee. Serve with Ghee Rice (see page 106) or Poories (see page 115).

3 tablespoons ghee
2 bay leaves
3 green cardamom pods
4 red onions, peeled and blended to a
   paste in a food processor
1½ teaspoons Ginger Paste (see page 12)
1½ teaspoons Garlic Paste (see page 12)
1 teaspoon ground turmeric
2 teaspoons ground cumin
20 king prawns, peeled and de-veined
   (the tail shell could be left on, if you
   prefer)
300ml (1¼ cups) coconut milk
4 green chillies, slit open lengthways
1 tablespoon salt
the tender coconut meat from 1 fresh
   coconut, chopped (optional)
1 teaspoon ground cardamom
½ teaspoon sugar (optional)

ACCOMPANIMENTS

LEMON RICE
GHEE RICE
TAMARIND RICE
TOMATO RICE
YOGHURT RICE
CORIANDER MASH
MUSTARD MASH
SPINACH TEMPERED WITH CUMIN
AND GARLIC
PICKLED CARROT, BEETROOT AND RADISH
CELERIAC AND MUSTARD SALAD
SPINACH AND COCONUT PORIAL
TAPIOCA CRISPS
CURRIED YOGHURT
WITH TOMATOES
SPICED ONION YOGHURT
SEENI SAMBAL
CHILLI AND GARLIC DIP
POORIES
SQUID INK AND SESAME NAAN
TAWA PARATHAS

ACCOMPANIMENTS

LEMON RICE

This is one of the best rice dishes from southern India. Fresh, light and fragrant, it looks beautiful and works very well with most fish dishes.

Wash the rice in cold running water once or twice. Place in a bowl of cold water and leave to soak for 25 minutes. Strain through a sieve to drain off all the liquid.

Bring 1 litre (4 cups) of water to the boil in a saucepan and add the rice. Cook, uncovered, for 8–10 minutes, until the grains are just tender. They do not need to be al dente but they should not be overcooked and mushy.

Drain through a sieve and set aside to cool. Heat the oil in a pan, add the mustard seeds, chana dal and urid lentils, if using, and let them crackle. When the chickpeas and lentils start to turn golden, add the curry leaves and turmeric. Reduce the heat and stir for 30 seconds, then mix in the salt and half the lemon juice. You may need to sprinkle in a little water to prevent the turmeric burning if the heat is too high.

Add the cooked rice and the remaining lemon juice and toss gently to mix well without breaking up the grains. The rice should be evenly coloured by the turmeric.

200g (1 cup) basmati rice
3 tablespoons vegetable or corn oil
1 tablespoon mustard seeds
1 tablespoon chana dal (split yellow chickpeas)
1 teaspoon white urid lentils (optional)
20 fresh curry leaves
1 teaspoon ground turmeric
1½ teaspoons salt
juice of 3 lemons

GHEE RICE

This is a simple rice dish enriched with ghee or clarified butter.

Wash the rice in cold running water once or twice. Place in a bowl of cold water and leave to soak for 25 minutes, then strain through a sieve to drain off all the liquid.

Bring 1 litre (4 cups) of water to the boil in a saucepan and add the rice. Cook, uncovered, for 8–10 minutes, until just tender, then drain through a sieve. While the rice is still hot, add the ghee and sea salt and mix well. Serve immediately. If you make it in advance, you can reheat it in a microwave.

250g (1¼ cups) basmati rice
1½ tablespoons ghee or clarified butter
1½ teaspoons sea salt

TAMARIND RICE

This traditional Hyderabadi rice dish is called puliara *in India. The hot, sweet and sour flavours work well with any soft fish.*

Wash the rice in cold running water once or twice. Place in a bowl of cold water and leave to soak for 25 minutes. Strain through a sieve to drain off all the liquid.

Bring 1 litre (4 cups) of water to the boil in a saucepan and add the rice. Cook, uncovered, for 8–10 minutes, until the grains are just tender. Drain through a sieve and set aside to cool.

Heat the oil in a large frying pan and add the mustard seeds. When they crackle, add the asafoetida, dried red chillies, chana dal and peanuts. Stir until they turn golden, then add the curry leaves and tamarind paste and cook for 2–3 minutes. Now add the ground chilli, turmeric, salt and sugar, reduce the heat and cook for 5 minutes. You should see the oil leaving the sides of the pan. Fold in the rice and mix carefully without breaking the grains. It is ready when the spices are mixed thoroughly and evenly throughout the rice.

200g (1 cup) basmati rice
100ml (scant ½ cup) sesame oil
1 teaspoon mustard seeds
¼ teaspoon asafoetida
3 dried red chillies
2 teaspoons roasted chana dal
20 unsalted peanuts
15 fresh curry leaves
200ml (⅞ cup) tamarind paste
1 teaspoon ground kashmiri chilli (or other chilli powder)
¼ teaspoon ground turmeric
1 tablespoon salt
2 teaspoons sugar

TOMATO RICE

This has a sharp, fresh flavour from the tomatoes and lemon juice and an attractive colour.

Wash the rice in cold running water once or twice. Place in a bowl of cold water and leave to soak for 25 minutes. Strain through a sieve to drain off all the liquid.

Bring 1 litre (4 cups) of water to the boil in a saucepan and add the rice. Cook, uncovered, for 8–10 minutes, until the grains are just tender. Drain through a sieve and set aside to cool.

Heat the oil in a large frying pan or a wok and add the mustard seeds. When they crackle, add the chana dal and stir till it turns golden. Add the curry leaves, then immediately add the onion and cook for 3–4 minutes, until translucent.

Now add the puréed tomatoes and stir-fry over a high heat for 3–4 minutes. Stir in the turmeric and the kashmiri chilli, then reduce the heat to low and cook for 5 minutes. Add the ginger, green chillies, tomato quarters, salt, sugar and lemon juice and stir-fry for 2 minutes. Fold in the rice, heat through and then sprinkle in the chopped coriander.

200g (1 cup) basmati rice
100ml (scant ½ cup) groundnut oil
1 teaspoon mustard seeds
1 teaspoon chana dal (split yellow chickpeas)
15 fresh curry leaves
1 onion, chopped
5 tomatoes, puréed in a blender, plus 1 tomato, cut into quarters
1 teaspoon ground turmeric
1½ teaspoons ground kashmiri chilli (or other chilli powder)
1cm (½-inch) piece of fresh ginger, finely chopped
2 green chillies, slit open lengthways
1 tablespoon salt
1 teaspoon sugar
2 tablespoons lemon juice
1 tablespoon chopped fresh coriander

YOGHURT RICE

Despite its bold ingredients, this dish has a soothing effect on the stomach, due largely to the alkaline quality of the yoghurt. You could enrich it by adding some pomegranate seeds, chopped cucumber or chopped raw mango – or even grated carrot for colour.

Wash the rice in cold running water once or twice, then place in a bowl of cold water and leave to soak for 25 minutes. Drain well. Bring 500ml (2 cups) water to the boil in a saucepan and add the rice. Cook, uncovered, for 12–15 minutes, until the rice is very soft; it should be a little overcooked. Drain and leave to cool.

Add the chillies, ginger, salt and curry leaves to the rice and mix in with a wooden spoon, mashing the rice a little with the back of the spoon. Now mix in the milk and yoghurt.

To temper the rice, heat the oil in a pan until very hot and add the mustard seeds. When they crackle, add the roasted chana dal and dried chillies. As soon as the chana dal turns golden, add the curry leaves and onion and sauté until the onion is brown. Pour this mixture on to the rice and leave to cool. Chill thoroughly, then serve sprinkled with the coriander.

200g (1 cup) basmati rice
2 green chillies, chopped
2.5cm (1-inch) piece of fresh ginger, finely chopped
2 teaspoons salt
5 fresh curry leaves, shredded
200ml (⅞ cup) milk
250g (1 cup) Greek yoghurt
1 tablespoon chopped fresh coriander

For tempering:
2 tablespoons vegetable or corn oil
1 teaspoon mustard seeds
2 teaspoons roasted chana dal
2 dried red chillies, broken in half
10 fresh curry leaves
1 red onion, chopped

CORIANDER MASH

A rich mash makes an excellent accompaniment to grilled or roast fish – even better when it's spiced, as in this recipe. The juices from the fish work as a sauce, to be soaked up by the mash.

Cook the potatoes in boiling water with the turmeric and salt until tender. Drain and push through a fine sieve into a bowl. Mix in the butter while the potatoes are still warm.

Heat the ghee or clarified butter in a heavy-based frying pan and add the coriander seeds, cumin seeds and red chilli flakes. When they release their aroma, add the ginger and green chillies. Add the mashed potatoes and stir to mix well. Add the cream and stir over a low heat until the potatoes absorb all the cream and leave the sides of the pan. Sprinkle in the coriander and lemon juice, mix well and serve.

500g (1 pound 2 ounces) floury potatoes, such as Desiree, peeled and cut into chunks
1 teaspoon ground turmeric
1 teaspoon salt
75g (⅓ cup) butter
1 tablespoon ghee or clarified butter
1½ teaspoons coriander seeds, roasted in a dry frying pan and then crushed
½ teaspoon cumin seeds, roasted in a dry frying pan and then crushed
½ teaspoon red chilli flakes
2.5cm (1-inch) piece of fresh ginger, finely chopped
2 green chillies, chopped
4 tablespoons single cream
2 tablespoons chopped fresh coriander
juice of ½ lemon

MUSTARD MASH

Mashed potatoes have been a popular accompaniment in Western cuisine for a long time but the addition of some Indian spicing has a great effect. This recipe uses mustard but you could experiment with your own combinations.

Cook the potatoes in boiling water with the turmeric and salt until tender. Drain well and push through a fine sieve into a bowl. Mix in the butter while the potatoes are still warm. Heat the ghee or clarified butter in a heavy-based frying pan and add the mustard seeds. When they begin to crackle, add the ginger and green chillies.

Stir in the mashed potatoes, then add the mustard and cream and mix over a low heat till they are well blended and the potatoes leave the side of the pan. Stir in the coriander and remove from the heat.

500g (I pound 2 ounces) floury potatoes, such as Desiree, peeled and cut into chunks
I teaspoon ground turmeric
I teaspoon salt
100g (7 tablespoons) butter
I tablespoon ghee or clarified butter
½ teaspoon mustard seeds
2.5cm (I-inch) piece of fresh ginger, chopped
2 green chillies, chopped
2 tablespoons Dijon or English mustard
2 tablespoons single cream
I tablespoon chopped fresh coriander

SPINACH TEMPERED WITH CUMIN AND GARLIC

This has a sharp, fresh flavour from tomatoes and lemon juice and an attractive colour.

Remove and discard the stalks from the spinach, then wash the leaves thoroughly to get rid of any grit. Drain and dry on kitchen paper.

Heat the oil in a wok or large frying pan and add the cumin seeds, followed by the garlic. When the garlic turns golden brown, add the spinach and sauté for a few seconds, until it begins to wilt. Add the salt and butter and mix till the spinach is completely wilted. Serve immediately.

500g (I pound 2 ounces) fresh spinach
I tablespoon vegetable or corn oil
I teaspoon cumin seeds
3 garlic cloves, chopped
a pinch of salt
20g (I½ tablespoons) salted butter

PICKLED CARROT, BEETROOT AND RADISH

A simple assortment of pickled vegetables, this makes an attractive garnish. The sharp flavour kick-starts the enjoyment of many a fish dish, especially tandoori dishes.

Peel the carrot into long, thin strips with a vegetable peeler, discarding the skin (alternatively slice it thinly lengthways on a mandoline). Prepare the radish in the same way. Peel the beetroot and slice it thinly on a mandoline. Wash it in cold running water several times until it stops leaching its colour. Put each vegetable in a separate bowl.

Put all the ingredients for the pickling liquor in a pan, bring to the boil and boil for 5 minutes. Cool slightly, then pour an equal amount over each of the vegetables. Leave in the fridge for 24 hours.

Drain off the excess liquor and mix the vegetables together. Sprinkle with the chopped dill and serve.

I large carrot
I white radish
I medium beetroot
½ tablespoon chopped dill

For the pickling liquor:
750ml (3 cups) water
450ml (1¾ cups) white vinegar
150g (⅔ cup) caster sugar
4 teaspoons salt
juice of I lemon
I tablespoon fennel seeds
½ teaspoon black onion seeds

CELERIAC AND MUSTARD SALAD

This makes a delicious accompaniment to grilled or steamed fish. The crunch of raw celeriac works particularly well with soft, delicate fish such as plaice or halibut.

Mix the mustard, mustard oil, salt, sugar, onion seeds and lemon juice together in a bowl. Peel the celeriac and cut it into fine matchsticks, then add it to the dressing and toss well. Chill before serving.

I tablespoon kasundi mustard or wholegrain mustard
I tablespoon mustard oil
½ teaspoon salt
½ teaspoon sugar
½ teaspoon black onion seeds
juice of ½ lemon
I celeriac

SPINACH AND COCONUT PORIAL

This is a traditional vegetable dish from southern India. The spinach stalks are used along with the leaves, giving the dish an interesting texture and mineral flavour.

Bring a large pan of water to the boil, plunge the spinach into it and cook for 1 minute, then drain. Run under ice-cold water to arrest the cooking and prevent discolouration. Squeeze out excess water from the spinach and set aside.

Heat the oil in a wok or large frying pan and add the mustard seeds. When they crackle, add the dried chillies and chana dal and fry until the chillies change colour. Add the curry leaves and onions and sauté until the onions are translucent. Stir in the ginger, green chillies and turmeric and stir-fry for a minute. Add the grated coconut and sauté for a minute. Add the salt and the blanched spinach and cook for 2 minutes.

250g (9 ounces) fresh spinach, shredded
3 tablespoons vegetable or corn oil
1 teaspoon mustard seeds
3 dried red chillies
1 teaspoon chana dal (split yellow chickpeas)
10 fresh curry leaves
2 onions, chopped
1cm (½-inch) piece of fresh ginger, chopped
3 green chillies finely chopped
1 teaspoon ground turmeric
50g (2/3 cup) grated fresh coconut
2 teaspoons salt

TAPIOCA CRISPS

Tapioca root (cassava) is available in Caribbean and Sri Lankan shops, sometimes even in supermarkets. It's really easy to make it into crisps, and it has a distinctive taste and texture, making it a much more interesting choice than potato crisps.

Heat the oil to 200°C/400°F in a deep-fat fryer or a large, deep saucepan. Peel the tapioca roots and slice into thin rounds, using a mandoline or a vegetable slicing attachment on a food processor. Quickly drop the slices into the hot oil one by one and stir with a slotted spoon to prevent them sticking together. Cook for about 2 minutes, until crisp and golden, then remove and spread them out on kitchen paper to absorb excess oil. Transfer to a mixing bowl while hot. Mix together all the seasonings, sprinkle them over the crisps and mix well.

oil for deep-frying
2 medium-sized tapioca roots (cassava)
2 teaspoons salt
1 teaspoon red chilli powder
a large pinch of sugar
a large pinch of asafoetida

CURRIED YOGHURT WITH TOMATOES

We had a recipe for curried yoghurt in The Cinnamon Club Cookbook *(Absolute Press, 2003) but this one has more upfront flavours and spicing. It works particularly well as a cold sauce.*

Heat the oil in a pan and add the mustard seeds. When they crackle, add the curry leaves the garlic and onion and sauté till the onion is translucent. Add the turmeric, ginger, green chillies and tomato and stir-fry for 2 minutes, until the tomatoes are just heated through but haven't disintegrated. Leave this tempering to cool, then sprinkle in the coriander and whisk in the Greek yoghurt, salt and sugar. Serve as an accompaniment to grilled fish.

2 tablespoons vegetable oil
I teaspoon mustard seeds
IO fresh curry leaves
2 garlic cloves, sliced
I red onion, sliced
I teaspoon ground turmeric
2.5cm (I-inch) piece of fresh ginger, chopped
2 green chillies, slit open lengthways
I tomato, cut into quarters
I tablespoon chopped fresh coriander
250g (I cup) Greek yoghurt
2 teaspoons salt
I teaspoon sugar

SPICED ONION YOGHURT

Essentially this is a raita – a cooling Indian dip or dressing. In this recipe I've reversed the proportions so there is a lot more onion than yoghurt. The result is much more intense than usual.

Put all the ingredients except the yoghurt into a bowl and mix well. Set aside for 2 minutes, then gradually fold in the Greek yoghurt.

2 red onions, finely chopped
2.5cm (I-inch) piece of fresh ginger, finely chopped
2 green chillies, finely chopped
I teaspoon salt
I teaspoon sugar
leaves from a sprig of mint, shredded
80g (⅓ cup) Greek yoghurt

SEENI SAMBAL

This Sri Lankan chutney will perk up almost any dish. It works just as well with chicken and other white meats as with fish. While most sambals are hot and sour, this is hot and sweet, cooked slowly to give a marmalade-style consistency.

Heat the oil in a heavy-based pan, add the onions and cook gently for a minute. Add the cinnamon stick, cardamom pods and curry leaves and cook until the onions turn pale golden. Now add the vinegar, red chilli flakes, salt and sugar and cook until the onions caramelise and turn golden brown. Remove from the heat and leave to cool.

3 tablespoons vegetable or corn oil
200g (7 ounces) onions, sliced
Icm (½-inch) piece of cinnamon stick
2 green cardamom pods
6 fresh curry leaves
I tablespoon white vinegar
2 dried red chillies, flaked
I teaspoon salt
2 teaspoons sugar

CHILLI AND GARLIC DIP

This spicy dip is based on the sauce that accompanies Tibetan momos in India. It also goes very well with fried snacks.

Drain the soaked red chillies, reserving the soaking liquid. Blend them to a smooth paste in a blender or food processor, adding a little of the reserved water if necessary.

Heat the oil in a heavy-based pan, add the garlic and sauté for about a minute, until soft but not browned. Add the chilli paste and cook over a low heat for 10 minutes, stirring occasionally. Add the vinegar and tomato ketchup and cook for 5 minutes. The dip should turn glossy and the oil should start to leave the sides of the pan. When this happens, add the sugar and salt, then taste and check the seasoning. If the dip is too hot, add an extra tablespoon of tomato ketchup.

30g (1 ounce) dried red chillies, soaked in 125ml (½ cup) warm water for at least an hour
100ml (scant ½ cup) vegetable oil
50g (2 ounces) garlic, chopped
4 tablespoons malt vinegar
2 tablespoons tomato ketchup
1½ tablespoons sugar
1½ teaspoons salt

POORIES

Poories are known as luchis *in Bengal, where they sometimes use a tad more oil or ghee to make the bread flakier. They also use refined flour rather than wholemeal, and add some onion seeds and carom to the dough, which makes the bread more flavoursome and easier to digest. Feel free to use wholemeal flour in the recipe below, if you prefer it.*

Poories make an excellent accompaniment to dry curries and are very popular with children as a snack or even as picnic bread.

Mix together the flour, salt, sugar and seeds. Rub in the ghee or oil with your fingers until it is well incorporated, then make a well in the centre of the mixture. Gradually pour in the water, mixing well to make a stiff dough. Knead until smooth, then cover with a damp cloth and set aside for 15 minutes. Divide the dough into 20 balls and cover again.

Heat some oil for deep-frying in a deep-fat fryer or wok. Take one of the dough balls, apply a little oil to it and roll it out with a rolling pin into a circle approximately 10cm (4 inches) in diameter. Repeat with the remaining dough, then deep-fry the poories in hot oil until they puff up and become crisp and golden. Drain on kitchen paper and serve.

500g (3⅓ cups) plain white flour or chapatti flour (or half and half)
2 teaspoons salt
1 teaspoon sugar
1 teaspoon carom (ajowan) seeds
1 teaspoon black onion seeds
1 tablespoon ghee or oil, plus 2 tablespoons oil for rolling
250ml (1 cup) water
oil for deep-frying

SQUID INK AND SESAME NAAN

MAKES 20

Everyone is familiar with naan bread but this is a very unusual way to make it. The jet-black naans topped with golden sesame seeds look very dramatic. They go well with spicy stir-fries, such as Orissa-style Stir-fried Squid (see page 46). Squid ink is available in sachets from some fishmongers or occasionally in bottles from speciality food shops.

Sift the flour, salt and baking powder into a bowl. Add the squid ink and rub it in with your hands. You might want to wear gloves, as the ink does stain the fingers! Whisk together the milk, sugar, egg and half the oil, add this mixture to the flour and knead lightly to make a soft dough (take care not to overwork the dough or it will become too stretchy). Cover with a damp cloth and leave to rest for 15 minutes. Pour the rest of the oil over the dough and turn it a few times so that it is evenly coated. Divide the dough into 8 pieces and roll out each one into a circle about 12.5–15cm (5–6 inches) in diameter. Sprinkle a few sesame seeds on top.

Heat a heavy-based frying pan, place a naan bread in it and cook over a medium heat for a minute or two, till the underneath is lightly coloured. Place the pan under a very hot grill for a minute or two, until the naan puffs up and the sesame seeds turn golden brown. Repeat with the remaining breads.

300g (2 cups) plain flour
I teaspoon salt
½ teaspoon baking powder
2 tablespoons squid ink
120ml (½ cup) whole milk
I tablespoon sugar
½ egg, lightly beaten
I tablespoon vegetable oil
I teaspoon sesame seeds

TAWA PARATHAS

MAKES 8

Triangular parathas like these are rarely seen in restaurants. Prepared in homes across northern India most mornings, they are an example of home cooking at its finest.

Mix the chapatti flour with the salt, oil and water and knead to make a smooth dough. Cover with a damp cloth or cling film and leave to rest for 15 minutes. Divide the dough into 8 parts and shape each into a smooth ball. Dust the work surface with flour and roll out each ball into a circle about 15–20cm (6–8 inches) in diameter. Now spread a little ghee or oil on top of the dough, sprinkle with a few seeds, if using, and dust with flour. Fold the dough in half to make a semi-circle. Repeat the same process of ghee, seeds and flour on the semi-circle and then fold in half again to make a triangle. Roll out the triangle carefully until it is about 3mm (⅛ inch) thick. Place a tawa or a large, heavy-based frying pan or griddle over a medium heat. Place the paratha on it and dry roast it for a couple of minutes, until the surface looks dry and brown specks start to appear underneath. Turn over and cook the other side until that, too, is speckled with brown. Brush the top lightly with ghee or oil. Turn the paratha over again and repeat the process; you should see the layers in the bread open up. Remove from the heat once both sides are golden and crisp. Repeat with the remaining pieces of dough, wrapping the breads loosely in foil to keep them warm while you cook the rest. Serve with a curry of your choice.

500g (3⅓ cups) chapatti flour, plus extra for dusting
2 teaspoons salt
I tablespoon oil
275ml (1⅛ cups) water
2 tablespoons ghee or oil
I tablespoon carom (ajowan) seeds or black onion seeds (optional)

INDEX

INDEX